To: John Hollar

Best Wishes !

Art Neal

Memory and Representation

Memory and Representation:
Constructed Truths
and Competing Realities

edited by

Dena Elisabeth Eber
and
Arthur G. Neal

Bowling Green State University Popular Press
Bowling Green, OH 43403

Library of Congress Cataloging-in-Publication Data

    Memory and representation : constructed truths and competing
realities / edited by Dena Elisabeth Eber and Arthur G. Neal.
       p.   cm.
    Includes bibliographical references.
    ISBN 0-87972-829-9 (cloth) -- ISBN 0-87972-830-2 (pbk.)
    1. Memory--Social aspects. 2. Symbolism (Psychology)--Social
aspects. 3. Mental representation--Social aspects. I. Eber, Dena
Elisabeth. II. Neal, Arthur G.

BF378.S65 M46 2001
153.1'2--dc21

                                                00-050829

Cover design by Chris Carnicom

CONTENTS

Introduction

MEMORY, CONSTRUCTED REALITY, AND ARTISTIC TRUTH

Dena Elisabeth Eber and Arthur G. Neal

Linkages between memory and representation give humans their distinctive characteristics and accounts for their dominance within the animal kingdom. The special human capacities include using symbol systems to construct the world around them, communicating with each other, and storing learned experiences. The use of symbols for making events coherent and predictable facilitated the pooling of group resources in problem solving. Remembering past events, through either narratives or direct experiences, permitted the development of systems of culture and facilitated the use of group resources for asserting mastery and control over events.

Symbolic meanings are derived from human consciousness and include the contents of our perceptions of the events in which we are engaged. Symbols are the raw materials from which we construct meaning in social life, and as such they consist of the words or gestures we draw upon to identify objects and events. Symbols are arbitrary in that there is no necessary or inherent reason for a particular symbol to represent any particular object or event. We construct meanings through the symbols we use because it is practical and expedient to do so, and we must have some level of agreement on the meaning words or symbols will have if we are to successfully communicate with each other.

Symbolic meaning is derived from the process of reality construction by which meanings, designs, and vocabularies are created for describing the external environment. Once created, such meanings are incorporated into personal spheres of thought and action. Although the cumulative experiences of a given group of people shape their basic design for living, it is the individual's definition of the situation that shapes the immediate course of action he or she is likely to follow. We live in immediate acts of experience, and on these experiences we impose a wide variety of symbolic meanings. In the ordinary course of events we are able to draw on the meanings others provide for us, but in many situations communal forms of understanding are not readily available. These circumstances require us to reflect on the meaning of social life and its practical implications for our existence.

Language and art are examples of such symbol systems and provide us the primary framework for constructing representations of the world around us. Our use of language shapes our reality perceptions, permits us to identify and classify objects, gives meaning to our experience, structures our social acts, and enables us to communicate with others. In addition to language, many artists express everyday personal and collective experiences through imagery, sound, or performance, thus adding another layer to reality construction and interpretation. We notice only a small proportion of environmental events in our everyday experiences; most we ignore or give only slight attention in passing. Through naming and labeling we create a symbolic universe, and the symbols we use become the central aspects of the reality we know and understand. In everyday life, the symbols we use and the objects they represent become blended inseparably in reality perceptions, in communication, and in social action. It is through such symbolic constructions that we are provided with a usable framework for shaping our memories and organizing them into meaningful lines of action.

The detached student of language may note that symbols are abstractions, substitutes, or vicarious meanings that stand for something else. The situation is quite different, however, when we look at symbols from the perspective of those who use them. The separation between a symbol and the object it represents is a distinction we tend to lose sight of in the course of our daily lives. We tend to blend the symbol and its referent into an inseparable pattern. Symbols make up a very large part of the stimulus environment for any social group, and we come to perceive symbols as having an existence in their own right.

Reality perceptions do not stem so much from the objective qualities of the physical world, but from subjective interpretations we impose on environmental stimuli. Humans may endow mountains, rivers, and stones with extraordinary qualities and sacred meanings, as they have at many times and places, or they may regard these aspects of the environment as prime examples of mundane and uninteresting things. Notions about the qualities of what exists are, in effect, ideas or cognition of what is real, what is possible, and what lines of action are appropriate. Peter L. Berger (1969) has described these cognitive processes in terms of the human tasks of "world construction and world maintenance." We create the world through our perceptions of it, and then seek to maintain the world in a style and manner consistent with our beliefs about it.

The concept of world construction refers to the realities created by humans through the invention of language, tools, social norms, values, and other aspects of culture. These realities are constructed out of the activities in which humans are engaged. But once created, these realities become endowed with factual qualities; they are experienced as objective; they are defined as the natural state of affairs. As social influences impinge on thought and action, the world constructed becomes two steps removed from the physical world. The first step involves the selectivity in constructing reality at the collective level, while the second step consists of additional modifications as individuals attempt to make sense out of their personal experiences.

World maintenance consists of the social influences, controls, and supports by which people uphold definitions of reality in any given social context. A great deal of repair work is required because both societies and individuals always remain unfinished products: People frequently pursue self-interests at the expense of the group's well-being; human efforts lead to frustration and failure; people sometimes make mistakes and do stupid things; it sometimes becomes necessary to deal with evil in human affairs. In the process of world maintenance, the social definitions of reality come to be defined as the ultimate realities of the universe and the basis for order in human affairs.

It is through such symbolic constructions that we are provided with a usable framework for shaping our memories and organizing them into coherent systems. But the words we use and the objects they represent are not identical. There is a physical world that exists independently of our perceptions of it. While we assume that our memories directly reflect past experiences and therefore are valid, empirical studies of the memory process fail to support this view (Waites 1997). We do not experience the world directly. Instead, our perceptions and experiences are always partial and incomplete. The recall of past events takes the form of memory fragments rather than complete narratives on the unfolding of events.

As John Dean noted during the Watergate hearings, "the mind is not a tape recorder." To this we may add that our minds do not provide us with photographic representations of the world. Instead, our attention tends to be focused only on the objects and events of immediate interest. All else is off limits and excluded in order to prevent our minds from becoming overloaded. To reduce clutter, only specific things are noticed or remembered within the total environmental matrix.

We tend to remember those things we have tagged as important to remember and to forget those things that are regarded as trivial. The eyewitness in courtroom proceedings is required to "tell the truth, the whole truth, and nothing but the truth." As conscientious as the eyewitness may be, this is not a reasonable possibility. This is especially the case if the event in question was not central to the focus of attention at the time an ongoing activity was interrupted. The selectivity of what we remember is shaped by a variety of variables. These include our prior experiences as well as our subsequent experiences; our mood state at the time the event occurred (Kuiken 1991), and our tendency to take memory traces and organize them into coherent narratives. We seek harmony, balance, and consistency in our personal lives, and we slant the memory process in order to achieve these results (Janoff-Bulman 1992).

Many forms of art have been and will continue to be integral to remembering narratives and personal experiences. How our culture embraces the truth of artistic "re-presentation" is one key to how we collectively remember our past. Through symbol systems such as language and art we construct a reality of the past that informs our present and provides the basis for our memory.

Questions about the nature of "truth" and "reality" are necessarily implicated in studies of memory and representation. According to the Webster dictionary (1996), truth is being true, and true, among other definitions, is faithful, loyal, and constant. In this sense, humans represent, or "re-present," the truth if they are faithful to their ideas and the content that they want to portray. Truth, then, is a meaning that comes from within. Webster also says that the state of being true coincides with fact, and that fact agrees with reality. From this definition, truth equals reality. For this book, truth is often, but not always, the same as reality. Reality is the state of being real, and real is factual or true in an objective way. Of course, that objectivity is through the eyes of the beholder.

In the final analysis, reality is a construction of the world that we build up through symbol systems such as language, mathematical models, and pictures. When humans experience new symbols and facts, they tie this information in with collective experiences. In so doing, the realities of the world are re-defined. New experiences are necessarily integrated with historical experiences that are transmitted from one generation to another (Mills 1963). From such dialectic, new realities emerge to subsequently become objective definitions that are both ratified and reified.

Uses of the Past

The dead, the living, and the unborn become linked not only through the transmission of genetic materials, but also through the transmission of a cultural system that gives meaning to persons, objects, and events (Ben-Amos and Weissberg 1999) Just as the transmission of genetic materials shapes our biological characteristics, the use of language and other symbols provides the raw materials for linking personal lives with each other and with environmental conditions. It is through the use of symbols that social order is created, the world becomes meaningful, personal identities are shaped, and individuals find their place within the broader scheme of human affairs.

The past is called into play when questions are raised and decisions must be made. The future may be anticipated, but it cannot be known in advance. Through shaping the course of action we wish to follow, we draw upon the only sources of information available to us. These include our personal experiences, which are limited, and the forms of awareness that are handed down from the past. Individually and collectively, we seek to repeat those activities that were rewarding to us in the past and to avoid those activities that were associated with pain and suffering. Those in trustee positions of authority draw upon such collective experiences as they set national priorities and seek to promote the collective good.

We typically think of memory as the retrieval of information that is stored in the brains of individuals. In the final analysis, however, the contents of the human brain are social in character. As Maurice Halbwachs (1992) told us many years ago, memory is collective. Throughout most of the human past, collective memories were transmitted primarily by means of an oral tradition. Stories were told about heroic times and how social life was created as a moral community. The continuity of social life was provided by oral traditions in which narratives were elaborated and embellished in order to have dramatic effects upon listeners. New generations were provided with guidelines on what to do and what to avoid in given situations. Then as now, storytelling and mythical accounts provided the ingredients for shaping personal and collective identities.

With the advent of civilization, writing greatly increased the memory capabilities of human beings. But, it was through the invention of the printing press that a major breakthrough occurred in the retention and distribution of information. During the middle fifteenth century, the German printer Johann Gutenberg (c. 1398-1468) set up a movable-type press, the basis for the modern press. The tedious work of the scribe had its limits, and this revolutionary invention made text, and thus information, available to the mass culture, knowledge previously limited to a privileged few. The mechanical reproduction of writing produced a quantum leap in the human capabilities for memory and representation (Benjamin 1969). Books and newspapers could now be produced in large quantities and distributed over large geographical areas, and at a lower cost than was previously possible. The archiving of written material was made possible in new and innovative ways. Libraries now became repositories of collective experience and wisdom (Traister 1999).

The memory capabilities of human beings were greatly extended through the many technological innovations of the twentieth century.

Today, we have newspapers, books, formal documents, photographs, recordings, television documentaries, videos, computers, and other devices that permit archiving data to be drawn upon when the need arises. Most significant among these technological innovations was the advent of the Internet. After the Gutenberg Press, we believe this innovation is the beginning of another great revolution in the dissemination of information, which will in turn shape realities and memory in ways still yet to unfold. We also believe that at the beginning of the twenty-first century there are still too many people in the world who do not have clean drinking water, let alone a computer and a modem to be a part of the Internet revolution; however, we see this changing in the future. The many forms of recorded history provide us with access to information about the problems of the past, how attempts were made to solve these problems, and the outcomes that followed. This vast amount of information, however, only has importance after it is interpreted, given plausibility, and constructed along lines to give applicability to present concerns.

Gaye Tuchman (1978, 3) observed that today we "learn basic lessons about social life from the mass media, much as hundreds of years ago illiterate peasants studied the carvings around the apse or the stained glass windows of medieval cathedrals." Tuchman maintained that, like any other society, our society must pass on its heritage from one generation to the next and prepare people for the challenge of changing conditions. Through popular history, as it is presented on television and in the movies, the past lives on in the present as a form of remembering. The remembering becomes important as a way of becoming informed of the basis for extraordinary accomplishments and extraordinary failures, lost opportunities and what might have been, inappropriate hopes and aspirations, and the role of chance happenings in human affairs. This is apparent in films such as *Titanic,* in which the events of the actual catastrophe were not only factually inaccurate, but were intertwined with a tragic love story, the details of which were a drama created for the screen. Even though the audience is aware of the drama, the viewers of this movie will forever associate, or rather remember this event with the movie in mind, thus collectively re-constructing a reality about the *Titanic* disaster. Patricia Reynaud's essay, "Simple Minds, Complex Distinctions: Reading *Forrest Gump* and *Pleasantville* through the Lens of Bourdieu's Sociological Theory" (chapter 7 below), addresses in-depth examples of the impact of film on mass society's memory.

The technical and stylistic features of television and the movies strongly influence the kinds of representations that are produced. In a successful production the viewers are drawn into the performance as they mentally take on the roles of the characters portrayed and identify with the situations created. In this process the many details and idiosyncrasies of the technology by which television is produced is of little concern or interest to most of the viewers. The scriptwriting, the rehearsals, the stage props, the photography, and the moving dots of light on an electronic screen recede into the background as viewers become engrossed in the symbolic events being portrayed. The self-attitudes, emotions, and predisposition of the viewers shape and refine the content and the entertainment value of television productions.

The realities of the past take on special meaning through our current perceptions of them, and the future becomes a mixture of present fears and aspirations. While our language separates time dimensions into past, present, and future, our experience tends to unify them as we reflect on the character of societal events. From audience experiences with media entertainment, the time dimension may be described as "everywhen." There were certain events that happened in the past that could also happen now and are likely to happen in the future. The time dimension becomes a form of eternal dreamtime in which individuals travel psychologically to remote places and respond to the activities of people who represent both the living and the dead.

The past becomes a form of selective memory, since the factual details of what happened in history often are neither known nor knowable. In portrayals of the Old West, the Civil War, or World War II, historical events become symbolic events that are used for reflections about the problems and challenges of contemporary living. Vicki Patraka's "Spectacular Suffering: Performing Presence, Absence, and Witness at U.S. Holocaust Museums" (chapter 8 below) is a look at how the Holocaust is represented as a symbolic event through museum displays. In mass entertainment, our memories can be anything we want them to be. The freedom to take the past and touch it up is evident in the work of scriptwriters, producers, performers, sponsors, and the viewing audience. All play their part in shaping the content of media productions. In the interplay among the agents shaping popular history, the distinction between fact and fiction is of little concern. Pseudo-events are elaborated as if they were real-life situations, and celebrities are created for winning audience identification with splendid displays and performances. Entertainment is promoted at the expense of historical accuracy.

In popular culture and mass entertainment, assorted themes are recurrent in the process of shaping collective identities and transmitting the social heritage. Accounts of political blunders reflect the incompetence of government officials; reports on crime stories reflect the problems of evil; reports on natural disasters reflect the vulnerability of humans to environmental forces. Specific events are simplified and personalized in order to make them coherent, while the vast array of activities covered confirms the complexity of modern social living. Awareness of societal happenings serves to validate the individual's everyday assumptions and to determine the need for modification and refinement of his or her understanding of events.

The philosopher George Santayana once said, "those who do not learn from history are condemned to repeat it." The problem of properly learning from history, however, is a difficult task. The proper way to remember becomes both a psychological and a political question (Kramer 1996). For example, why have both the media and the public-in-general become preoccupied with the deaths of Marilyn Monroe, Elvis Presley, President Kennedy, and Princess Diana? Heightened emotional arousal and intense identifications have accompanied the troubled lives and tragic deaths of these celebrities. By way of contrast, there has not been a comparable level of identification with the millions who died in the Nazi Holocaust, the Soviet purges, or the influenza epidemic of 1919.

The sounds and images preserved on film, in photographs, and in recordings serve to perpetuate the immortality of celebrities and the excitement presumed to surround their personal lives. The images of celebrities who are now dead become frozen in time, surrounded with manufactured fantasies, and lacking in the reality checks that are connected with the aging process (Dixon 1999). The famous dead become our new saints by transcending the limitations of an earthly existence. It is through collective myths that we share our common humanity and gauge our mortality (Campbell 1988).

The televisual industries are geared toward promoting a sense of community through creating products that will have universal appeal, regardless of race, class, gender, or religion. In developing an appeal to the largest viewing audience, the common language becomes one of spectacle through the use of violence and destruction (Dixon 1999). These are attention-getting, transcend the mundane qualities of everyday life, and are enhanced through the visual effects that can be generated by modern technology. It is within this context that the audience becomes the primary determinant of the content of what is produced and also the judiciary which shapes the commercial success of any given production.

The linkage of memory with representation provides the raw materials for the construction of both personal and collective identities. Who we are, how we relate to others, and our perceptions of society are shaped through the use of language and other symbols derived from the social learning process. We typically respond to the question "who am I" by enumerating and evaluating social locations in categories such as age, sex, race, marital status, religion, occupation, family, and community (Neal 1983). The multiple aspects of an identity suggest that in modern society we are exposed to competing demands and obligations. Who we are and what we are to become are products of our experiences and how we process our memories over an extended period of time.

In popular thinking, memory is typically regarded as the retrieval of information that is stored in the brains of individuals. Such a view places a primary emphasis upon cognition and the rational capabilities of humans to recall stored information when there is an interest in doing so. This view is seriously flawed in several ways, as we will demonstrate throughout our analysis. For now, let us observe that the basic flaw stems from the failure to acknowledge the many ways in which the brain is embodied within an organism. The brain does not exist in a free-floating vacuum. Instead, the brain is embodied and serves as an intricate part of an organic system. But it is not the total system. Instead, it is required to work in concert with the rest of the body in a functionally interdependent manner. Dena Eber's essay, "Virtual Imaginations Require Real Bodies" (chapter 5 below), addresses the embodiment of knowledge in further detail.

Reality Construction

We assume in our everyday life that it is sufficient to know something about the general style of events in order for us to manage and control them. We make purchases in stores without knowing how the merchandise is produced. The workers who produce the commodities we buy never enter into our field of vision, and we only rarely think about the human labor or the technology that produces the objects we use. In this respect, we tend to draw boundaries around the objects of concern to us. We typically think of steak as an item obtained from the supermarket and seldom reflect on either the manner by which beef is produced or the imagery surrounding the slaughter of animals.

Most of us drive automobiles without knowing very much about how they operate mechanically. We are aware of the proper steps and procedures to follow in driving a car, and for most of us this is adequate. It is usually sufficient for us to know that if we flip a switch the light will come on. In doing so, we are unlikely to ponder the nature of electricity, how it is produced, or the technical principles upon which it works. Our daily lives are then oriented toward the objects of interest and guided by a general knowledge of the procedures to follow in achieving the goals we seek. The dependability of knowledge permits us to proceed in a matter-of-fact fashion in those situations that are understood to be normal, routine, and standardized.

Decisions on what is real, what is valid, and what is possible increasingly depend on judgments by experts and specialists. We do not all share the same realities because we employ different vocabularies, and we are limited in our capacities for grasping the many realities important to us. The emphasis on credentials and certification qualifies experts for making pronouncements about truth. But as John Tomlinson (1999, 56) has observed, "all experts are lay people most of the time and in most areas of their lives." As a result, personal vulnerability is inherent in modern social living because all of us, including experts, are characterized by only partial and incomplete knowledge of most of the events in which we are engaged.

The limitations of personal knowledge stem from the size and complexity of the symbol systems that prevail in the modern world. Most of the meanings conveyed by the more than 600,000 words in the English language are understood by only small subgroups of the larger population. A lawyer, for example, may readily understand the specialized vocabulary another lawyer uses, but those outside the legal profession probably will not. And the medical terminology of doctors is so far removed from everyday speech that the physician sometimes has difficulty explaining the results of medical diagnosis in a language the patient can understand. Sometimes college graduates can engage in lively conversations about the ideas of Shakespeare or Camus but confront difficulties in grasping the language of an income tax form or the provisions of an insurance policy. The use of specialized vocabularies by subgroups of the population provide grounds for mutual understanding and shared meanings within the group, while excluding all who are nonmembers.

From the vantage point of the individual, however, it is not necessary to develop a grasp of all the technical vocabularies that shape and influence our lives. This would not be possible. Instead, we tend to orient our daily lives around a general understanding of the event in which we are engaged and to regard precise and detailed knowledge on the inner working of things to be the task of specialists. For example, it is not necessary for us to develop a grasp of the terminology needed to understand the principles on which the telephone works; it is only necessary to know how to call the repair person when the phone is out of order.

In the scientific community, truth claims are based on the use of empirical methods for obtaining either verification or falsification of a particular hypothesis. The use of agreed-upon methods are assumed to provide a basis for approximating the realities of the external world. Truth claims then become conditional in that they are based upon specific forms of measurement, data collection, and data analysis. A further requirement is that the research findings of any particular study be amenable to replication by an independent investigator. In the final analysis, however, truth claims are established on the basis of consensus or agreement within the scientific community. Despite consistency in measurement and the replication of results, many findings are, over time, found to be false, mostly because the basis from which the standards are measured or interpreted changes. Even with a sound basis for objective analysis, it is up to the investigator ultimately to select, decide how to analyze, and finally present the data. Leaving information out or using various methods of analysis may completely change how the data is interpreted, which in turn results in a constructed "objective" reality. In the larger society, the veracity and usefulness of the scientific method depends on the extent to which scientific knowledge can be utilized in achieving technological solutions to specific, identifiable problems.

In the courtroom, it is the use of proper organizational procedures that provides the basis for determining "objective truth" in establishing guilt or innocence in any given case. Yiwei Chen's "Reconstructing the Reality: Unwanted Memory in the Courtroom" (chapter 4 below) addresses this issue in further detail. Judicial procedures are designed to promote the discovery of truth by separating the role of the prosecuting attorney from the role of the defense attorney. The prosecuting attorney is obligated to prepare a brief that will represent the interests of the state in determining the facts of the case and obtaining a conviction, while the defense attorney is obligated to represent his or her client by selectively presenting facts for establishing innocence. The judge is obligated to preside impartially over the proceedings and to invoke his or her authority in deciding what is central and what is peripheral to the adversarial proceedings. Through the social interactions of the prosecuting attorney, the defense attorney, the judge, the witnesses, and the jury, it is presumed that "objective truth" will prevail. However, in such a quest, selective perceptions and multiple realities operate throughout the courtroom proceedings.

The facade of justice and impartiality becomes evident in the practice of plea-bargaining. Negotiations between the prosecutor, the defense attorney, and the accused often lead to a plea of guilty to a lesser offense. For example, a defendant initially arrested on an armed robbery change may agree to plead guilty to a charge of unarmed robbery. The bargain results in an easy conviction for the prosecutor and in leniency for the accused. Obtaining convictions through the process of plea-bargaining compromises the veracity of the judicial process and violates the moral emphasis upon universal standards of justice in our court system.

In the plea-bargaining process the parties involved are concerned not so much with determining the facts of the case as with constructing a form of reality that will be mutually satisfactory. The courts face the general problem of obtaining convictions to certify the effectiveness of the criminal justice system. Obtaining a conviction through a plea of guilt to a lesser offense provides a basis for "closing the books" in any given case. In achieving this, court hearings are structured in such a fashion as to deny the transaction that has occurred. When pleading guilty to a lesser offense, the accused is required to testify that he or she is making the plea voluntarily and is actually guilty of having committed the offense for which prosecution is being sought. All parties are explicitly aware that official realities are being negotiated during the plea-bargaining process (Scheff 1968).

Artistic Truth

Visual imagery is one symbol system which humans use to embody memory. Through this they express, understand, represent, and ultimately construct reality. As a result, an understanding of the truth in art is key to grasping the veracity of memory and representation. Burton Beerman and and Celesta Haraszti's *"Jesus' Daughter*: Memories of Child Abuse Represented through Performance" (chapter 6 below) addresses performance as a visual system of language in the quest for artistic truth.

The expanded use of digital images in movie making, television productions, advertising, and the digital arts clearly indicate that modern forms of consciousness are shaped by constructed images that are designed to have some intended effect on others (Baudrillard 1988). Yet to make these observations is to go beyond the digital images themselves. However, it is the investigation of digital imagery that helps us understand the core of artistic truth (Eber 2000). Such images represent some of the dominant forms of imagery that prevail in our time and place. These include the constructed images from movie making, from television production, from advertising, and from other signs and symbols in our consumer-oriented society. Images are positively simulated to promote the encouragement of desire and to offer promises of pleasure and self-fulfillment.

The key to seeing artistic truth through digital imagery is to understand its connection with photography and film. Because many digital images and films appear to be photographic, or photographic-like, the medium forces artists and viewers to reconsider the photograph as a representation of physical reality. In turn, this rethinking influences how they see reality and truth in the artistic symbol system.

Although those that study images understand that a photograph is not a physical truth, digital images make this assertion clearer. Nonetheless, many artists and viewers still often react as if photographic representation of physical reality is in essence truth. Digital image making affords the ability to construct a photographic-like image. As artists and viewers see the connection between the notion of photographic and of digital construction, it encourages them to reconsider truth.

As Roland Barthes (1972, 1980) explained many years ago, the photograph is not a direct reflection of the external world. Photographic images are neither physical reality nor even copies of reality. Instead, both the human eye and the camera are selective in what is emphasized, and the meaning of what is seen or recorded is taken out of context. The qualities of the camera, the film, the perspective of the photographer, and the manipulations that occur in the darkroom shape the selectivity. While many viewers assume that photographic images are truthful representations, students of images clearly understand that the photograph is not a direct reflection of the physical world (Eber 2000).

Susan Sontag (1977) suggested that although the photograph contains a trace of the physical world, it is also an interpretation, no more or no less than that of a painting. Like Sontag, we believe that a photograph is no closer to physical reality than that of a painting, but further, we believe that the only physical truth an image contains resides with the viewer and the artist. Truth in imagery is an expression and recognition of the artist's and the viewer's lived experiences or personal expressions. It is thus a truthfully rendered construction of reality, as truthful as a symbol system can portray. Prior to photography, the mass population understood art to be a truthful expression that embodied a kind of reality, but they understood that reality to be one of many. Like science, photography and film are too often embraced as objective reality. An investigation of art from the period prior to photography will clarify this notion.

Constructed Truth in Pre-Photography: An Example

It is only since the invention of photographic processes that society has concerned itself with physically real representations in photographic imagery, depictions they see as the truth. Prior to that, what an artist created was understood as *a* reality, and it often served as a narrative, a constructed truth from the point of view of that artist. For one such artist, David, this often meant a political message or a lesson, a reality he wanted to portray. In Jacques Louis David's *The Death of Marat* (1793), he depicts the assassination of a man named Marat, a close friend of David as well as a leader in the Reign of Terror that preceded the French Revolution.

At the time of his assassination, Marat was very ill and spent much of his day in a medicated bath with his head wrapped in sheets. Despite his handicap, he equipped the tub with a makeshift desk and conducted everyday business from it, which included seeing visitors. One such visitor was Marat's assassin, Charlotte Corday, who, after killing Marat, was immediately arrested and executed (Canaday 1981).

In his painting of the story, David did not depict Charlotte Corday, nor did he show any portion of the assassination. Instead, David made a passionate painting of his friend Marat, depicting him as a defenseless sick man in a medicated bath. He portrayed an innocent soft face and a body with a vulnerable gesture, showing sympathy over Marat's death. David was uncharacteristically romantic, yet expressed his utmost truth, the view and emotion of a life experience. This was David's constructed truth.

Others did not show the same reality of this event. A. Scheffer, a romanticist born after the assassination, showed the scene quite differently. Scheffer painted the arrest of Charlotte Corday, a romantic rendition, but compared to *The Death of Marat,* emotionless. Scheffer had no immediate experience with this event, he was not part of the revolution that led up to it, and he had nothing but stories to know of it. The depiction was at best a metaphor for one of Scheffer's personal experiences, but was most likely a retelling of this story. The two renditions of the Marat assassination were true, but each depicted a different reality, each a constructed truth from the view of the artist and his life experiences.

Viewers who saw these images understood that they were both true renditions of events through different eyes. Photographers, filmmakers, and television producers use this same construction process; they choose tools to construct a truth based on their reality. Recording devices such as cameras do not record the visible; they record something we otherwise might not see. "It is not a visual truth, it is an objective record, but one which has to be interpreted in the light of additional information" (Gombrich 1980, 182). Thus, a skillful photographer will understand the objectivity of her medium, much like a painter understands how paint sits on canvas, and uses it to mold her subjective reality, her truth. We maintain that digital artists do the same: they use an objective mathematical model and pixel information to show the truth of their lived experiences and the collective experiences of all humans.

Conclusion

What it means to be human has become more clearly evident through modern discussions of the fantasies and the visual imagery so prominently emphasized in the modern world. The so-called hyper-realities of digital societies, such as television, movies, and other media constructions of reality, are central to these discussions. In the final analysis, all realities are perceived and communicated through the uses of symbols. As Dena Eber's essay explains, "virtual reality," as with all other forms of reality, involves a complicated mixture of sensory experience synthesized with symbolic meanings. We draw upon a combination of personal memories with stylized forms of cultural representations to construct the realities of the world around us.

We use symbols and our imaginations to make sense out of the world, and once these representations become embedded in our memories, we tend to reify them. We create beliefs about life and death, about the basis for justice, and we invent systems of religion. But once these things are created and become a part of established traditions, they tend to be endowed with objective, factual qualities. In effect, through the process of reification, we create an objective, factual world that in reality is only a product of our imaginations.

In the shopping mall or in the supermarket, we encounter "virtual realities" that have been embellished to reflect the sacred qualities of our consumer lifestyles. The distinction between denotative and connotative meanings breaks down, as do previous distinctions between objective and subjective truth. Hyper-reality is reflected in designing oranges to be more orange-like than the real orange; injecting steaks with chemical substances to make them look more steak-like than the real thing; playing soft and soothing music to reduce tension levels among shoppers.

In the final analysis, memory and representation become essential ingredients in the myth-making process. We typically look upon myth as "a false belief." In reality, however, we do not actually know whether most of our beliefs are true or false. The important thing about myth is not its truthfulness or falseness, but whether or not we believe in it (May 1991). The meaning that our ideas hold for us is what sustains us in finding a purpose in life and in selecting the means that are necessary for attaining the goals of interest. As Joseph Campbell (1988) so eloquently pointed out, through myth the mundane world becomes embellished with spiritual and sacred qualities.

Works Cited

Barthes, Roland. 1972. *Mythologies*. Trans. Annette Lavers. New York: Hill & Wang.

——. 1980. *Camera Lucida: Reflections on Photography*. Trans. Richard Howard. New York: Hill & Wang.

Baudrillard, Jean. 1988. *Selected Writings*. Ed. Mark Poster. Stanford, CA: Stanford UP.

Ben-Amos, Dan, and Liliane Weissberg, eds. 1999. *Cultural Memory and the Construction of Identity*. Detroit: Wayne State UP.

Benjamin, Walter. 1969. "The Work of Art in the Age of Mechanical Reproduction." *Illuminations*. New York: Schocken. 217-52.

Berger, Peter L. 1969. *The Sacred Canopy*. Garden City, NY: Anchor.

Campbell, Joseph. 1988. *The Power of Myth*. New York: Anchor.

Canaday, J. 1981. *Mainstreams of Modern Art*. Fort Worth: Holt, Rinehart & Winston.

Dixon, Wheeler Winston. 1999. *Disaster and Memory*. New York: Columbia UP.

Eber, Dena. 2000. "The Student's Construction of Artistic Truth in Digital Images." *Digital Creativity* 11: 1-15.

Gombrich, E. 1980. "Standards of Truth: The Arrested Image and the Moving Eye." *The Language of Images*. Ed. W. J. Mitchell. Chicago: U of Chicago P. 181-217.

Halbwachs, Maurice. 1992. *On Collective Memory*. Ed. Lewis A. Coser. Chicago: U of Chicago P.

Janoff-Bulman, Ronnie. 1992. *Shattered Assumptions: Towards a New Psychology of Trauma*. New York: Free.

Kramer, Jane. 1996. *The Politics of Memory*. New York: Random House.

Kuiken, Don. 1991. *Mood and Memory*. Newbury Park, CA: Sage.

May, Rollo. 1991. *The Cry for Myth*. New York: Dell.

Mills, C. Wright. 1963. *Power, Politics, and People*. New York: Ballantine.

Neal, Arthur G. 1983. *Social Psychology: A Sociological Perspective*. Reading, MA: Addison-Wesley.

Scheff, Thomas J. 1968. "Negotiating Reality: Notes on Power in the Assessment of Reality." *Social Problems* 16: 3-17.

Sontag, Susan. 1977. *On Photography*. New York: Anchor/Doubleday.

Tomlinson, John. 1999. *Globalization and Culture*. Chicago: U of Chicago P.

Traister, Daniel. 1999. "'You Must Remember This . . .'; or, Libraries as Locus of Cultural Memories." *Cultural Memory and the Construction of Identity*. Ben-Amos and Weissberg. 202-30.

Tuchman, Gaye. 1978. "The Systematic Annihilation of Women in the Mass Media." *Hearth and Home: Images of Women in the Mass Media*. Ed. Gaye Tuchman, A. K. Daniels, and J. Benet. New York: Oxford UP. 3-38.

Waites, Elizabeth A. 1997. *Memory Quest: Trauma and the Search for Personal History*. New York: Norton.

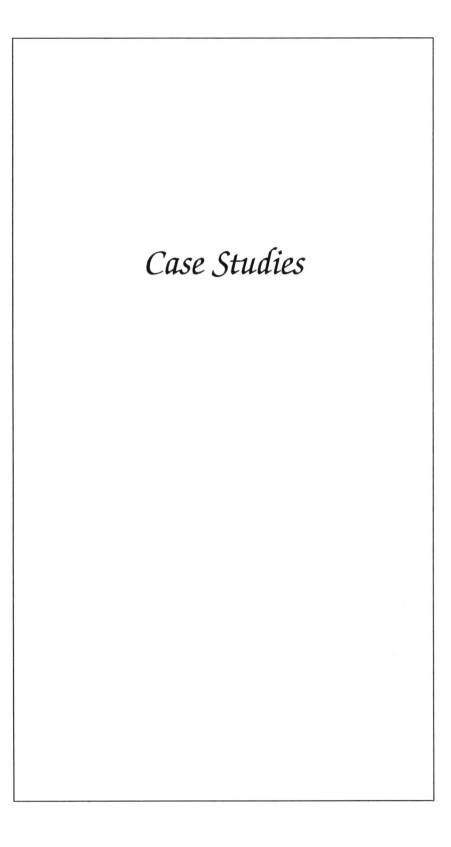

Case Studies

1

ANCESTRAL DREAMS:
RE-LIVING THE PAST, RE-CREATING THE FUTURE

Rebecca L. Green

Between late June and early October, the highlands of Madagascar come alive with music, dance, feasts, politically-based theatrical performances, flowery oration, cattle wrestling, singing, and art as Merina and Betsileo families celebrate life, family, identity, and accomplishment. Roads fill with groups journeying home to join the festivities, often accompanied by an ancestor or two who will be re-enshrouded and re-entombed during *famadihana* reburial ceremonies.

Elaborate relationships between the living, their ancestors, reburial ceremonies, and weaving comprise elements integral to the highland Malagasy cultures of the Merina and Betsileo peoples. The interplay of these cultural elements demonstrates a complex world of spiritual power, social significance, and potent symbolism. This chapter addresses the creation, manipulation, and perpetuation of individual and collective memory; the articulation and representation of identity that is manifest through this; and the careful negotiation of the pervasive and elaborate funerary practices and ancestral relationships in Madagascar's central highlands. In particular, I will focus on people's relationships with their ancestors, relationships based upon the creation, use, and transformation of *lambamena* burial shrouds and the *famadihana* reburial ceremony system in which they are employed. See figure 1 for an example of a ceremony.[1]

Issues
The importance and interconnectedness of tangible and oral cultures, memory, and identity is key in studying memory and representation. Memory of one's culture, of important cultural actors, and of actions and interactions of and between the actors can be used to create identity: personal, familial, community-based, ethnic, and national. In particular, oral histories, which are created from verbalizing and perhaps manipulating personal or group memories, can perpetuate culture and

Fig. 1. As the first, and eldest ancestor is removed from the tomb, the family pauses momentarily while the band plays the Malagasy national anthem (1993).

thus identity, which is tied closely to one's cultural environment. In highland Madagascar, verbalizing, recounting, and performing narratives of ancestral interactions perpetuates the ancestors, thereby keeping them alive. As long as one's ancestors are alive, one is empowered and given the tools with which to negotiate one's position in society.

Ancestors are powerful because rather than simply remaining in the past and linear, they are three-dimensional. By three-dimensional I mean that ancestors occupy three planes of existence simultaneously, incorporating elements of the past, present, and future. Ancestors lived in the chronological past and it is through mental and physical memories that the living remember them. They also exist in the present, in that they are believed to live in a universe parallel to that of the living. The ancestors are thought to continue in death whatever occupation they performed in life. Thus, descendants planning an ancestral ceremony must warn their ancestors not to leave the tomb to go to work because the ancestors' attendance is essential to ensure the success of the ceremony. Ancestors also represent the future, for not only do they continue to survive long after their mortal bodies have perished, but without them and their benedictions, the destiny of the living is thrown into doubt.

Because of the ancestors' three-dimensionality, the relationships between the living and their ancestors are both circular and reciprocal. The circularity of ancestral relationships stems from the polyvalent qualities accorded ancestors as they evolve from living being to omnipotent Ancestor. The reciprocal nature of the relationship is based on the fact that the successful transition to Ancestorhood depends on the living correctly caring for their ancestors, who will reciprocate with benedictions and good will, as I will discuss later. The significant issue for the ancestors in relation to reciprocity, however, is to be remembered. Conversely, the primary issue for the living is to remember, because memories are the tools by which the living can create specific representations of their ancestral history and their involvement in it, and thus take an active role in manipulating their past, present, and future.

There is more than one way to remember. In fact, as noted by the linguist Charles L. Briggs (1986), "some messages can only be transmitted nonverbally." Thus, additional issues that I consider significant in relation to memory and representation are the concepts of embodiment and body memory. Moreover, traditional modes of production, exemplified by the weaving in figure 2, and ritual, such as the reburial ceremonies displayed in figure 3, are actions repeated over time and become examples of body memory. Through this process and repetition, they become reproductions of mental memory and thus of knowledge.

Fig. 2. Hélène Raheliarisoa sitting at her framed loom, on which she is weaving indigenous *landibe* silk. Note the cooked *landibe* and skeins of spun *landibe* hanging from the ceiling (1993).

Fig. 3. Once re-enshrouding is complete, family members gather around the ancestor to touch and interact with him or her (1993).

As individuals manipulate and negotiate their remembrances and body memories, which are extremely powerful modes of imprinting memory, social and cultural responsibility and accountability are paramount. To maintain memories is one thing, what one does with them is another. Ancestral interactions, and the memories and narratives relating to them, are extremely powerful and, like fire, can be deadly if mishandled. The scope of danger varies. For example, it can be socially disastrous if community members judge one's handling of a situation as irresponsible and inappropriate, while it can be physically dangerous if the ancestors themselves are angered. But the rewards for proving oneself responsible and accountable by acting appropriately and fulfilling one's social and ancestral obligations are immense. Thus, if ancestral interactions are told and retold skillfully and provide the proper interpretation of a situation, the narrator can greatly empower him or herself. Similarly, a strong relationship exists between memory and actual physical objects, the latter having the potential to be significant mnemonic devices, as do hand-woven burial shrouds, such as *lambamena,* shown in figure 4, in highland Madagascar.

As an art historian exploring the individual memories and interpretations of ancestors and traditions upon which highland Malagasy culture is based, I focus particular attention on relationships between artistic expressions and sociocultural negotiations as expressed in the manipulation of identity and power. I do not mean power in the sense of political rulership or domination, but rather power as a force that is personally, socially, and culturally enabling. Power is a multifaceted, multicentered force that is grounded in the sociocultural environment and includes human, superhuman, natural or environmental, and supernatural elements. It is also integral to the communicative and ideological environment through which it is understood and given meaning in order to locate it within one's experiential background. It is a force that allows individuals to perform actions by which they can gain control of their lives, realize their ultimate potential, and transform their world.

In understanding people as active agents who form and create their own realities through actions, conversations, and relationships that empower, I draw on a multidisciplinary theoretical framework addressing issues of the individual, agency, and the dynamics of change. Michael Carrithers (1990), Warren D'Azevedo (1973), Henry John Drewal (1984), Margaret Thompson Drewal (1992), Ivan Karp (1986), Patrick R. McNaughton (1988), Anya Peterson Royce (1982), and others emphasize the active and interactive roles of individuals and the importance of context in the conception, creation, and use of art in understanding a culture and its art. Thus, I look to artists, consumers, and cultural

Fig. 4. Elders with the financial means often buy or weave the shroud to be used for their own funeral, in which case the shroud is called *lamba vato,* or *lambam-bato.* Bebe Razanamioly (1993).

and ritual experts as agents of action in economic, political, religious, and social networks and as manipulators of sociality. I use Karp's definition (1986, 137) of *agent* as one who exercises "power in its primary sense of the 'bringing about of effects'" and of *agency* as the "'causal power' through which we realize the potential of the world." I use Carrithers's definition (1990, 203) of *sociality* as the "power to create, maintain, and change forms of social life," a power that arises from an individual's inventive and imaginative creativity.

The establishment and successful manipulation of memories and relationships in highland Madagascar is contingent upon effective communication and dialogue within and between the worlds of the living and of the dead. Communication is crucial in establishing identity because it allows individuals to take active roles in their lives through enabling the dissemination of knowledge: of needs, desires, and requests. Knowing the questions being asked means that one is armed with the knowledge to satisfy the needs and is therefore empowered. The continual retelling of the encounters experienced between partners in this relationship further emphasizes the critical nature of dialogue. Continued and sustained dialogue creates a relationship that can award rights of family and ancestry, but likewise can demand responsibility, particularly responsible and intelligent negotiations of those rights.

Responsibility and accountability are paramount in highland Malagasy ancestral culture. Individuals are often challenged by ancestors, family, and community and they are given "tests" that they must satisfactorily pass in order to maintain the identity that they have cultivated and upon which they have built their lives. Tests include demonstrating appropriate behavior in certain ancestral situations, performing the correct ceremonies at particular junctures in one's life, and maintaining faith in one's ancestors in the face of a crisis or adversity. Such was the case for one group of siblings who tried to re-enshroud their long-deceased father, but due to a mistake made by the elders in charge of removing the ancestors from the tomb during the reburial, the siblings wrapped the wrong ancestor. The adult children were then in the unenviable position of having to redress the situation to appease their angered father, yet not offend their family elders.[2]

While failure to pass ancestral tests can result in serious consequences such as adversity or failure, epidemics, or even death, satisfactory performance results in empowerment. The status of individuals who prevail during crisis situations and who prove their political and social savvy as demonstrated by skillfully manipulating narratives is greatly increased. The living are empowered when they create ties to ancestry through experienced memory that affirm, realign, create, own, and manipulate identity. Ties to kinship and one's ancestral history provide a foundation with which to construct identity. Creating a representation of oneself for others to view and understand involves utilizing shared histories, vocabulary, and narratives to demarcate boundaries within which actions and events are located. By using shared or recognizable histories and narratives, a narrator contextualizes the experiences, making them relevant, familiar, and thus more meaningful.

One of the fundamental effects of the orchestration of habitus is the production of a common sense world endowed with the *objectivity* secured by consensus on the meaning (*sens*) of practices and the world, in other words the harmonization of agents' experiences and the continuous reinforcement that each of them receives from the expression, individual or collective (in festivals, for example), improvised or programmed (commonplaces, sayings), of similar or identical experiences. (Bourdieu 1986, 80; emphasis in original)

This historicizing and identifying oneself is evident in the experiences of highland Malagasy people who repeat and reenact narratives of ancestral interactions and is relevant to the work of the anthropologist Ruth Benedict and others. Benedict notes, for example, that "peoples' folk tales are . . . their autobiography and the clearest mirror of their life" (Benedict 1931, qtd. in Babcock 1995, 112). Moreover, as Benedict further notes, "what is communal about the [folklore] process is the social acceptance by which the trait becomes a part of the teaching handed down to the next generation" (Benedict qtd. in Babcock 1995, 112). Thus, narratives of highland Malagasy ancestral dreams or visions are repeated and reenacted across generational and existential boundaries. For, like Anthony Giddens's theory that the reproduction of structures creates them and can change them, Benedict stresses that "the power of the human imagination to make, remake, and reflect upon reality" (Benedict qtd. in Babcock 1995, 133). Similarly, performance theorist Margaret Thompson Drewal (1992, xiii) emphasizes the human agency in performance's reflexive and transformative properties, noting that creative transformation is accomplished through "repetition with critical difference" by agents who, rather than simply repeating a performance, improve upon it, individualize it, and *signify it* (Henry Louis Gates, Jr. qtd. in M. Drewal 1992, 4) to make it meaningful.

Thus, memories are created by repeated reenactments or re-visitations of events, tales, histories, or occurrences. Repetitive storytelling of the past re-creates, solidifies, and even *creates* the veracity of events and individuals. Continual retelling allows individuals to emphasize certain elements of a history and to magnify and sometimes distort certain passages of one's life, causing the narratives to become integral components of the teller's and audience's life and determining factors in the negotiation of identity.

Rituals, rigid procedures, regular formalities, symbolic repetitions of all kinds, as well as explicit laws, principles, rules, symbols, and categories are cultural representations of fixed social reality, or continuity. They present stability and continuity acted out and reenacted; visible continuity. By dint of repetition they deny the passage of time, the nature of change, and the implicit extent of potential indeterminacy in social relations. Whether these processes of regularization are sustained by tradition or legitimated by revolutionary edict and force, they act to provide daily regenerated frames, social constructions of reality, within which the attempt is made to fix social life, to keep it from slipping into the sea of indeterminacy. (Sally Falk Moore, qtd. in Turner 1986, 78)

Individuals use rituals and their predictable repetition as vehicles through which to negotiate identity within a particular context. As Sally Falk Moore notes, even within the strict societal rules that provide an event's contextual basis, there exists "a certain range of maneuver, of openness, of choice, of interpretation, of alteration, of tampering, of reversing, of transforming" (qtd. in Turner 1986, 79).[3]

Repeated public enactments of ceremony, tradition, and ritual are forms of theater or performance. It is the theatrical nature of public cultural events that gives them dynamism. While predictable on many levels, the human component of public *enact*ments ensures that they also provide malleable frameworks within which actors may create or re-create themselves and their social roles. One's identity and social reality are neither static nor constant, but pliable, having a plasticity that allows one to form certain personae for public consumption. Performance theorist Dorinne Kondo (1995, 49-50) observes that "the live aspect of theatre is critical. Live performance not only constitutes a site where our identities can be enacted, it also opens up entire realms of cultural possibility, enlarging our senses of ourselves in ways that have been . . . especially powerful." Thus individuals with an awareness of themselves, their roles, and their ability to manipulate their roles within society can carefully orchestrate and create the context of an event to produce the desired effect upon the audience and other actors. The creation of a "scene" is equally important during a reburial ceremony as during a Broadway play because in both the performance "illuminate[s] the truth of the post-structuralist dictum of 'no fixed text,' for even subtle changes in acting, intonation, lighting, blocking, . . . stage business or design . . . shaped, even totally changed, meaning" (Kondo 1995, 50-51).

Equating important cultural ceremonies and rituals with drama or theater is not new. Perhaps the most famous individual to comment on the performative aspects of social interaction is Shakespeare in his famous phrase "all the world's a stage" (*As You Like It* 2.7.114). Using Victor Turner's definition of a social drama or ritual as "the performance of a complex sequence of symbolic acts," performance specialist Richard Schechner notes that such acts "are inherently dramatic because participants not only do things, they *try to show others what they are doing or have done*; [so that] actions take on a 'performed-for-audience' aspect" (Schechner 1986, 74-75; emphasis in original).

Ancestral Reburials: Famadihana

The specific constellation of performative and cultural ceremonies to which I now turn are those of highland Madagascar, a culture that revolves around the ancestors. Recognized as the progenitors of culture and the creators of tradition (*fomban-drazana*), ancestors form the basis on which highland identity is established. Relationships with one's ancestors are reciprocal. Ancestors can be extremely active in the lives of their descendants if they so desire. It is imperative for the living to attentively care for and tend to the needs of their ancestors because Merina and Betsileo peoples believe that their ancestors are the source of all good fortune; yet if provoked or displeased by ill-treatment or neglect by their descendants, they can cause ill-fortune. Thus, filial obligations are fulfilled during ancestral ceremonies, the main point of interaction between the worlds of the living and the dead. One such ceremony is the *famadihana*.

Famadihana are reburial ceremonies during which the living re-envelope their ancestors in indigenous silk shrouds as seen in figure 3. The *famadihana* is a fundamental and intricate component of central highland Malagasy culture. It is not only a "living tradition" in that it continues to be practiced and to evolve in the ever-changing Malagasy world, but it is a "tradition for living," because it is through the *famadihana* that the living interact with their ancestors, physically and emotionally. It is this interaction that enables the living to understand their ancestors, and provides them with the experiences through which to interpret and reinterpret the past and present and to manipulate their future destinies, as I will discuss. Ancestral interactions are a source for narratives, told and retold by the living about the family, the community, themselves, and the dead, thereby creating one's social and communal identity.

Famadihana are a focal point for interaction that crosses worlds and generations. This ceremony enables the living and dead to care for one another by providing for each others' needs. It allows highland families to remain in contact with all their family members, living and dead, and gives them an opportunity to interact physically, emotionally, and spiritually. Consequently, it is a forum through which Merina and Betsileo people create and maintain their social, cultural, religious, and ethnic identities. For all of these reasons, *famadihana* are considered by many Malagasy to be the foundation of highland Malagasy culture.

Famadihana make existence possible for both the living and the dead. Ceremonies take place every two to twenty years and last one to four days, during which the ancestors are re-enshrouded, given gifts, spoken to, touched, carried, danced with, performed for, and generally interacted with under the close eye of family elders and a diviner. *Famadihana* are magnificent events with feasting, architectural and sculptural renovation, professional and amateur theatrical and political performances, presentations of gifts between hosts and guests, performances of elaborate and flowery speeches, invitation-only parades by family members and close friends who wear matching clothing, including accessories such as a purse, stockings, shoes, sunglasses, and wristwatch to demonstrate family unity, and general festivities for the entire community. An example of this is displayed in figure 5. The smallest *famadihana* that I attended had about forty participants, while the largest had over one thousand. They are fun, and at the same time, are also dangerous. If the ceremony is done properly, the ancestors will reward their descendants with benedictions. If it is done improperly, the ancestors will become angry and punish them. Either way, reburials are discussed, critiqued, analyzed, embellished, and created and re-created through narratives and recountings often years after an event takes place.

One of the primary components of a reburial involves enveloping one's ancestors in new shrouds, silk cloths that are wrapped around the existing ancestor bundle without removing the old shroud, as shown in figure 6.[4] Highland Malagasy shrouds are an ancestor's clothing and protection, and a source of his or her dignity and honor. The shroud is the tangible point of contact between the living and the dead. By interacting with the cloth, family members imbue it with requests for benedictions, requests that are then communicated to the ancestors as they are enshrouded in the cloth and empowered by it. Requests may ask for specific benedictions, including success in a business venture, or general blessings for a prosperous life. Interacting with the cloth also allows the ancestors' power to pass to their descendants. Thus, through the shroud, benedictions are conveyed, fertility granted, and success assured. Therefore, within the contexts of the ceremony, the living are given the opportunity to create themselves anew, by fulfilling their duties to their

Fig. 5. The ultimate matching ensemble for women includes a suit, handbag, nylons, pumps, purse, hair tied up in a knot, and a *lamba* scarf around the shoulders (1993).

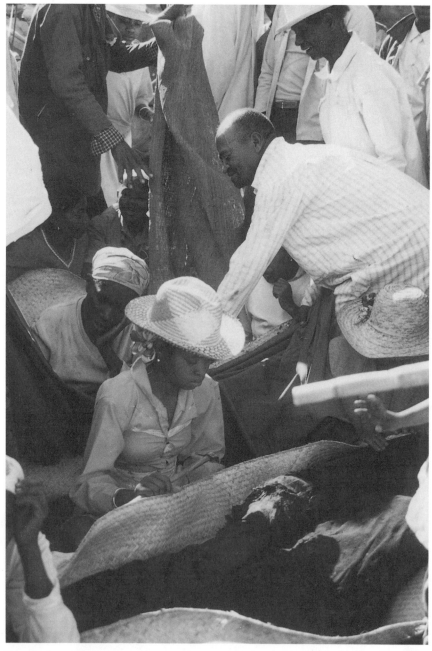

Fig. 6. Once the ancestors are carried out of the tomb, they are placed on the laps of women, who talk with them and cry over them before they are given their new shrouds (1993).

ancestors and by publicly performing this private family interaction before the critical eye of the community, thereby establishing a cultural and community reputation.

The ancestors remain "ancestors" as long as their needs to be sufficiently clothed and thus protected, kept warm, and honored are cared for. If they are neglected and forgotten, they will cease to exist. However, as long as their needs are met, as long as they are maintained within the family tomb, and as long as they are remembered and honored as individuals, they are happy and continue to exist as powerful beings. By wrapping the ancestors in burial shrouds during a *famadihana* reburial, the living supply their ancestors with the things they require to "live" such as clothing for warmth, bestow honor and respect upon them by ensuring they are not clothed in rags and by presenting them with filial gifts, and actually create and perpetuate their ancestors. Over the years, as the textiles and the ancestors' physical remains disintegrate, it becomes impossible to separate the two. As the ancestors turn to dust, the "ancestors" become a mixture of their remains and their silk shrouds, which become an indivisible element of those whom they were made to honor.

Eventually, individual ancestors are combined, during subsequent reburials, within a single shroud to create ancestral bundles such as those displayed in figure 7. At this point, memories of explicit individuals fade and the ancestors enshrouded within the bundle become omnipotent "Ancestors." Ancestors, which I designate with the capital "A," are omnipresent beings no longer associated with one individual ancestor, who no longer have the same needs as their mortal descendants and thus no longer require care.

Ancestral power is often experienced indirectly, as when a person encounters positive or negative fortune. The circumstances may be general, such as "nothing is going right" or "everything is going right," or specific, such as a test is failed or passed or a sick person dies or recovers her health. Thus the living depend upon their predecessors' goodwill for success, progeny, and good fortune. Raymond Decary (1962) documented a reburial held in 1918 to appease the host family's sixteenth-century founding ancestor, who was angry with his descendants and instigated an epidemic of cerebral-spinal meningitis as punishment. As soon as the family discovered, through divination, the epidemic's cause, they held a *famadihana* to re-envelope their ancestor in new silk *lambamena* to satisfy him.[5]

Clearly, the ancestors are powerful beings that command respect because of their ability to affect the lives of the living. Moreover, because family affiliation defines one's relational ties within one's com-

Fig. 7. Two separate ancestors are bundled together during a Merina *famadihana* reburial ceremony. Each is re-enshrouded separately before a final shroud is wrapped around both bundles, creating an "ancestral bundle" (1990).

munity, ancestral power also derives from their role as the ultimate family: past, present, and future. The location of the family's ancestral home and tomb is the *tanin-drazana* or the ancestral land, which provides the tangible basis of one's identity and is the first piece of information asked of a new acquaintance. The common question asked upon meeting someone for the first time is not "where are you from," but rather, "where is your family tomb?" Identity based upon a common homeland and ancestry, implying a common historic, culture, and tradition base, is powerful. Because ancestors serve as a link to or focal point of highland Malagasy identity, a person who cannot claim ancestral ties or support, who does not have ancestors as a referent on which to base relationships with the living, and who has no physical ties to an ancestral tomb is without access to this power and is thus powerless him or herself. An example of the family tomb is displayed in figure 8.

As a means of showing that they are able to tap into this powerful source of identity, many highland Malagasy report interacting with their ancestors. For diviners, who are highly trained individuals versed in ancestral tradition, communication, and interpretation, the interaction may be constant and direct. The late Ratsizafy, a powerful diviner, told me how an "alarm clock" rang in his head every morning to wake him before the sun rose so that he could stand under the stars and converse with his ancestors. Most people, however, communicate only periodically with their ancestors through dreams and visions. For these people, dreams establish a foundation for a relationship based on the memory of an ancestor and of each subsequent dream-based interaction. The dream sequence, as I encountered it among my friends and colleagues, occurs only once; the one story is repeated over one's life. But memory perpetuates the experience, embellishing it and using it to create and legitimize one's identity. Moreover, it is continually used as a foil against which later episodes or events are compared.

Memory thus plays an important role in the relationship with and creation of one's ancestors, and through them, oneself. Because highland Malagasy people base their identity and sense of self on the existence of and continued connections and interactions with their ancestors, it is by looking to their past, embodied in their predecessors, that the living anticipate and create their present and their future. However, the past itself is open to interpretation, resulting in varying traditions being followed within particular regions, generations, families, or individuals. "At every moment, and especially in the redressal of crises, the meaning of the past is assessed by reference to the present and, of the present by reference to the past; the resultant 'meaningful' decision modifies the group's orientation to or even plans for the future, and these in turn react

Fig. 8. Dada Koto and family on top of their ancestral tomb (1993).

upon its evaluation of the past" (Turner 1986, 98). Thus, ancestral narratives are continuously told and retold to establish an ancestral connection that can then be manipulated and interpreted as the living negotiate identity.

More than any other cultural element, intimate ancestral relationships and reburials are what Merina and Betsileo people say make them who they are. Without celebratory ancestral events and shrouds, which are the tangible representations of one's ancestors, highland Malagasy would not be Malagasy. Nor would they be Merina or Betsileo. Nor would they be considered human beings. In fact, without shrouds, they would be no better than dogs, the remains of which can as easily be thrown carelessly and disrespectfully into the woods rather than treated respectfully. Because Merina and Betsileo peoples, however, create their particular identities through participation in ceremonies and traditions honoring their ancestors, this fate is avoided. With each reenactment of an ancestral ceremony, and of reburials in particular, members of the family and community renegotiate their identities: as family members and community members; as fathers, mothers, and children; as conscientious, moral, and socialized human beings who are fully civilized members of society; as Merina or Betsileo; and as Malagasy. Each reenactment is essential to cementing and reaffirming these ties, to forging new relationships, and to creating new social, political, familial, and community-based positions and responsibilities. Thus, a highland Malagasy person is able to create and transform his or her particular identity through interpreting and reinterpreting one's past, one's ancestors, and one's traditions.

Ancestral Communication
Effective ancestral communication is essential. Without it, as I have mentioned, the living will not be able to request forgiveness for past faults or benedictions for future happiness from the ancestors, nor will the ancestors be able to reward or reprimand the living for their actions or inactions. The living communicate with their ancestors by consulting diviners, making offerings to them at ancestral altars or family tombs, conducting private prayer and public oration, and especially through performing the expensive and complex reburial ceremony during which they can actually touch their ancestors while talking with them. Ancestors, on the other hand, communicate with their descendants either directly through dreams and visions or indirectly through manipulating their descendants' fortunes. While indirect ancestral communication is arguably the most common interaction, it often lacks clear definitions or boundaries, and can be difficult to identify with certainty or through a

compelling "story-line." I focus here on direct ancestral communication, which is much more striking or notable due to its relative rarity in someone's life and due to the exacting nature of the encounter.

Direct communication occurs when ancestors contact descendants individually, generally by waking them at night or appearing to them in dreams. During such episodes, an ancestor relates the advent of disturbing situations, explains certain occurrences, discusses the extent of a descendant's transgressions, gives opinions on important issues, or describes an upsetting situation and indicates the steps necessary to alleviate the problem. The unusual nature of direct communication from one's ancestor makes it the source of powerful narratives the living use to establish their own identities, empower themselves, and negotiate their relationships within family and community.

Ancestral narratives usually revolve around particular ancestors or particular tombs. For example, one story relates that if a certain tomb develops a hole, no rain will fall in the region, giving proof of the ancestor's great power. Many people I spoke with said they did not *initially* believe that ancestors contacted their descendants through dreams until it happened to them. However, regardless of whether someone believes the accounts are true, virtually everyone knows at least one story of an ancestor communicating with his or her descendants.

The weaver Miriam Razanadrabe told me about the time her dead brother contacted her to complain that his clothing was dirty and needed to be washed. In her dream, she refused his request. Her brother returned in subsequent dreams insisting that his clothing be washed. The weaver eventually related her dreams to the rest of her family, who immediately recognized that her brother was trying to communicate that his clothing, or his burial shrouds, was in rags and that he must be in disreputable attire, cold, and required new shrouds. They called the extended family together and planned a reburial, which was judged successful due to the fact that the woman's brother no longer appeared in her dreams (personal communication, 1992).

In another example, a woman who did not initially believe in ancestral dreams was herself visited on three successive nights. The first night, her mother appeared and said that the family tomb was damaged by water, described the exact location and extent of the damage, and insisted that the ancestors housed within it were cold and that the structure must be repaired and the ancestors given new shrouds. The woman did not believe in dreams so she ignored it. The next night, her mother contacted her a second time and repeated her request for a *famadihana* reburial. Although the woman began to feel uncomfortable, she remained skeptical and ignored the message. Her third dream, however, worried her.

During this final dream, she was visited by her father, who had been buried in a different tomb than her mother. He scolded her, demanding "why have you disobeyed your mother!?" The woman became alarmed and quickly called the family elders together to discuss the situation. At the gathering, she learned that a cousin had similar dreams involving his parents, who share her mother's tomb. After hearing the testimonies of the woman and her cousin, the entire family went to the tomb to investigate. They found a hole in the tomb wall and water damage, exactly as their parents had described. This discovery convinced the woman that dreams are real and that the ancestors possessed tremendous power, and she and her family immediately began planning a reburial.[6]

One narrative told to me by Mr. Razafimahefa, an elder Merina shroud vendor, related how a woman he knew was contacted by her long-dead father. She awoke in the middle of the night to see her father standing by her bed. He told her that he was lonely and needed to be transferred to the family tomb. Her father, a road construction worker, had died about fifty years earlier a great distance from the family home and had been interred in a provisional grave. Unfortunately, the family did not know the location of his grave and therefore had been unable to transfer him to the family tomb to join the rest of the ancestral family. While oral memory is essential to the creation and continuation of ancestral identity and well-being, it is not enough. Physical location is also imperative. To remain buried alone, far from the ancestral tomb, and forgotten is a terrible fate because it means that the deceased will eventually cease to exist without the possibility of becoming an Ancestor. In the vision, the woman's father revealed the name of the town where his remains were located. The woman related this information to the rest of her family, which sent a delegation to retrieve her father. However, upon arrival, the woman and her family were still unable to locate the precise location of her father's grave. That night, he appeared to his daughter a second time, telling her to find an old man living in a large house on the road to a nearby town and to follow this man's instructions. The family set out again and, following the directions given in the dream, found the old man, who admitted knowing their late father. To their surprise, he was able to produce their relative's identity card. The old man then led them directly to the grave, from which they were able to recover his remains and inter him with the rest of his family (personal communication, 1993). In this case, not only was the ancestor's power related through the retelling, but the essential difference between ancestors, Ancestors, and oblivion was underscored. The woman's father was an ancestor, a remembered dead who could tinker in his family's lives, but had yet to achieve omnipotent Ancestor status because he was buried alone and had not been combined into a multi-ancestor bundle. He was threatened with oblivion if he did not attain the family tomb and the company of the other family ancestors soon.

An extremely powerful form of interaction between the living and dead is tactile communication. Through touch, the living and dead firmly and physically establish the historic family bond and ground themselves within the established familial and social community. Moreover, while many forms of communication can relay information and requests, tactile interaction is the most immediate form. For example, women often drape a new shroud across their breasts and womb while walking to the tomb or dancing in front of it during a reburial, as seen in figure 9, to convey the bodily region requesting an ancestral gift, or they sit with the ancestors on their laps and talk to them during reburials, as shown in figure 6. Moreover, if the living do not touch and rewrap their ancestors in new shrouds, it is said the ancestors will no longer know their descendants nor be able to give benedictions.[7] In addition to physically communicating familial love, honor, and respect, physically interacting with one's ancestors ensures their relative immortality because through touch, the living continue to experience and know their ancestors. Touch provides a direct and tangible link that reinforces and gives credence to ephemeral memories. This tradition of periodic physical interaction with the dead in turn reassures the living that they too will live forever. As noted by Jorgen Ruud (1960, 184), in highland Madagascar "life beyond lasts as long as the relatives and their descendants commemorate the dead, and one way of showing the dead that he is still an object of thought and affection is to wrap his bones in a new *lamba mena* which necessitates touching him." The necessity of touch in remembering and honoring highland Malagasy ancestors is echoed by the anthropologist David Graeber (1995, 264) when he states that "remembering the ancestors becomes a matter of handling corpses."

Physical interaction demonstrates convincing proof of one's bond, whether friendly or antagonistic, with another individual and is evident in narratives linking the living with their past. Many dreams involve ancestors communicating physically with a descendant. For example, immediately after having performed a *famadihana* for her husband, one woman was awakened when her late husband hit her on the head and yelled "*Vehivavy alika*," or bitch! The extreme insult was warranted because the family had re-enshrouded the wrong ancestor during the reburial. Due to the mix-up, he had received a poor-quality shroud brought by another relative and intended for someone else. Her husband was incensed. The cheap quality of the shroud he received meant that it would probably not last until the next reburial ceremony, and that his

Fig. 9. Noeline Rason dancing with a new *lambamena* shroud during a *famadi-hana* reburial ceremony (1993).

remains could be lost. His widow could not ignore such a violent physical and verbal exchange. She called the family together and convinced them, as well as the president of the local government, to authorize the reopening of the tomb to complete the ceremony properly and to the satisfaction of *all* the ancestors.[8]

This narrative brings up another important issue, that of the responsibility of the living family to provide the dead with sufficient shrouds. Everyone requires a shroud at burial, even if it means the community must provide it, because as one highland saying notes, "you are a human being first, and an enemy second." Moreover, the number and quality of shrouds offered provides the living the opportunity to renegotiate social hierarchies. A high-quality shroud elevates the giver's status within the family, living and dead, and the community, all of whom carefully scrutinize the ceremonies to judge individual fulfillment of social and moral responsibility.

Many ancestral narratives and interactions are recounted through physical interpretations or reenactments of tactile or body memories that bring the events closer to the reality of an individual's present situation. Body memory incorporates the remembered sensations, actions, and reactions of physical interaction, which have a strong effect on memory because the physicality of a situation increases the power of a mental memory arising from it. Not only does the person remember the event through his or her cognitive memory, but the body retains a memory of its own, a recollection of the physical interaction, the pain or comfort of the blow or caress that it can relive periodically by re-experiencing the sensation. As noted by Pierre Bourdieu (1986, 94), in "treating the body as a memory . . . [individuals] entrust to it in abbreviated and practical, i.e. mnemonic, form the fundamental principles of the . . . culture."

Of course, not all tactile interaction is as violent or as aggressive as the ancestor forcefully striking his widow on the head. Most narratives of ancestral contact focus on a verbal exchange and an ancestor's physical nearness; an ancestor enters the room, stands by the bed, or perhaps gently touches his or her living descendant. However, communication instigated by the ancestors is generally motivated by their perception that the living have behaved inappropriately or unwisely, prompting a reprimand. The level of physicality corresponds to the severity of the person's supposed transgression, which is then filtered through the personality of the particular ancestor.

In many cases, ancestors let their wishes be known through non-intrusive actions, often attributed as miracles and demonstrations of the ancestors' immense spiritual power. For example, one elder, Mr. Razafimahefa, recounted how a group of ancestors communicated their displeasure at being transferred from their old tomb to a newly built tomb. One displeased ancestor created an astonishing phenomenon during the transfer; to the amazement of the family, water poured from his dry corpse during the journey. One month later, to make their desire perfectly clear, a number of the ancestors appeared in dreams of those who had transferred them and warned, "you must return us to our tomb immediately! If not, you will die!" For some reason they did not want to be in the new tomb, and were prepared to make their descendants pay for their discomfort. The family quickly transferred their ancestors back to their original tomb (personal communication, 1993).

In a similar example, a diviner explained to me how his ancestor, a powerful diviner in his own right, had a long-running feud with the patriarch of a neighboring noble family. In fact, before his death, Raintamaina had made it clear that he must be higher than, and have his feet turned toward, the head of his rival Ngahimaro, whose tomb is located to the south of Raintamaina's. In fact, he wanted to insure that he would never be in an inferior position to Ngahimaro. Raintamaina's power was so great, that he communicated his continuing hatred of his rival to his sons by performing a miracle when they transferred his remains to his newly built tomb. When they attempted to pass near Ngahimaro's land, Raintamaina's remains became very heavy, too heavy to carry, because he did not want to go near the land of his enemy. According to Raintamaina's wishes, as conveyed through his bodily reactions, or his body memory, his sons were forced to take another route to avoid Ngahimaro's land altogether.[9] His wishes and desires were firmly embedded in his sons' mental and body memories as well, since they physically experienced his awesome power.

Ensuring the ancestors' happiness also includes making sure they are fed and entertained. Nourishment is usually provided symbolically, when guests attending an ancestral ceremony are fed in the ancestors' stead. It is said that when invited guests partake of good food and entertainment, so do the ancestors, who have also been invited and who participate vicariously through the living. Periodically, however, narratives describe a more literal feeding of the ancestors. The weaver Alfoncine Razanamalala, for example, described a large *famadihana* sponsored by a noble family in the countryside near Arivonimamo during which the ancestors' mysterious power was demonstrated in front of the numerous guests. The family hosting the ceremony decided that symbolically feeding the ancestors was not enough and that they needed to be fed literally as well. Therefore, after the ancestors had been wrapped in new shrouds, the hosts placed rice, bananas, and cups of water on top of the *lambamena* near the ancestors' mouths. To the amazement of the guests, the food and water disappeared. I was told that because the guests never left the area, they would have seen the host family tampering with the ancestral meal if that indeed had occurred. Thus, the consensus was that because no one witnessed tampering, it must have been the ancestors themselves who devoured the meal (personal communication, 1993).

It is the ancestors' great and mystical powers, as demonstrated by these mysterious feats, benedictions, and blessings, that are recounted and remembered throughout ancestral ceremonies and that the living contemplate. Moreover, due to the ancestors' powers, and to their ability to use these powers if they disagree with their descendants' actions, the ancestors are consulted over all important issues or decisions being considered by the living, are shown the results of actions taken, and are thanked for their support. Thus, a family will consult their ancestors on the advisability of making a significant purchase, and once the purchase is made, the ancestors may be approached to bless it. When the Malagasy family into which I was adopted[10] moved into a new home, we performed a ceremony to mark the transition and to invoke ancestral blessings. We kneeled and crouched in the ancestral northeast corner of the building's main room while the building's owners and a few key members of the extended family stood over us to give speeches, blow water to deliver blessings,[11] and pour libations in the name of the ancestors so that we, as the new tenants, would live prosperously in our new home. Similarly, when my fictive brother-in-law bought a used truck, a tremendous expense for a rural farmer and merchant, the entire family met at the ancestral tomb. Speeches were made, libations given, blessings of safe passage and profitable use pronounced over his new vehicle, and the happy owner drove away, blessed in his purchase by his entire family, living and ancestral.

Yet, interaction with the ancestors and their power is potentially dangerous because power and strength in and of themselves are not naturally beneficial unless controlled. If power is controlled successfully, it can cure illness, wash away pollution, restore the balance of existence between the living and the dead, and transmit ancestral benedictions. Uncontrolled power, on the other hand, can harm, injure, or cause illness. Therefore, while much of the interaction between the living and the dead addresses the communication of information, or identity, and feeling, or respect, in return for empowerment, some interaction is also concerned with controlling and limiting ancestral power so that it does not become harmful. Ancestral interaction can be very dangerous because gaining a clear understanding of what the ancestors want and how they will react to situations and actions can be difficult. In fact, judging whether an action is inappropriate or unwise can be difficult to determine until it is too late. This is one reason why highland Malagasy families consult diviners to help determine the appropriate course of action in order to avoid punishment.

Diviners, as in figure 10, are individuals who have apprenticed themselves for many years in the arts of divination, which is based on herbalism, color symbolism, and astrological, calendric, and numeric forecasting. They are experts versed in ancestral traditions and prohibitions, have direct access to the ancestral world, and can communicate at will. Two examples given to me related how diviners helped families negotiate seemingly impossible situations. In the first case, the family of a Betsileo woman was adamant that upon her death, her remains be interred in *their* family tomb rather than her husband's. Her husband, on the other hand, was resolute that she be included in his family's tomb rather than her family's. Neither side was willing to cede the issue. The only mutually acceptable solution, arranged after consulting a diviner, involved periodically transferring the woman's remains between the two tombs. Consequently, the deceased woman was interred first in her husband's tomb, moved to her family's tomb during their next *famadihana* celebration, and subsequently transferred back again as part of his family's next reburial. In this way, the woman's remains alternate between two tombs. Although this was the most agreeable solution at the time, implementation was not easy. It required continual communication and negotiation between the two families while organizing their respective *famadihana*. While unusual, this solution is not new nor excessive. The historian Guillaume Grandidier (1891, 316-17) mentions a similar situation at the end of the nineteenth century.[12] A recent predicament recounted to me resulted in an even more extreme measure. This time the controversy involved a dispute between two Merina women over the body of their mutual husband. Each woman wanted to bury her husband in her family's tomb. The final solution involved cutting the man in two and allowing both wives to inter half of her husband, a solution to which both women, and apparently the ancestor, were amenable.[13]

When placed in a cultural context, this seemingly gruesome solution is not as horrific as it may first appear to an outsider. The essential ancestral being, the soul, is located in an ancestor's bones, the *tolambalo*.[14] It is therefore imperative to wrap all the bones within a shroud to preserve that ancestor's soul. Moreover, the issues of primary importance, pleasing the ancestors and maintaining recognizable ties with them, thereby enabling them to give their living descendants good fortune, legitimacy, heritage, and identity, are realized only when the ancestors' remains are preserved in one's family tomb. Yet, as long as the bones are contained, they need not be treated delicately. In fact, the

Fig. 10. Ratsizafy, a *mpanandro* diviner, with his wife (1992).

bones are said to be the ancestors' essential physical manifestation *because* of their durability and are usually danced with vigorously during reburials, as shown in figure 11. Thus, in the case of the divided body, the important issue was dealt with; the ancestor's essence, his bones, was preserved, even if in two separate locations. In both instances noted above, the families were able to maintain ties with the disputed ancestor, thereby allowing the living to negotiate a particular identity based upon the ancestral history housed within their tombs. By maintaining a physical ancestral presence, the living maintain a tangible, bodily link to their ancestors and the memories about them. In much the same way that memories can be bolstered and framed by the existence of a tangible photograph, ancestral physical presence, interaction, and memories are important, essential even, in the creation and perpetuation of identity and of self in highland Madagascar.

Conclusion

Narratives and ritual promote the social continuity of life as it is known and understood in highland Malagasy cultures. Ancestral memories drive or inform the perception of identity for Merina and Betsileo peoples. People manipulate memories by recounting ancestral narratives to orchestrate ancestral involvement, thereby manipulating their status within the communities of the living and the dead. Ancestral accounts, dreams, or stories are testaments to the ancestors' power, and tests of the descendants' abilities to handle crisis and to turn a crisis into an opportunity for good fortune. Narratives are told and retold to prove one's link with the past and thus act as legitimizing forces that "authentic[ate] experiences and relationships" (Ong 1995, 355). They demonstrate the importance of the individual to that ancestor, who has gone to the trouble of contacting him or her, and provide an opportunity for the narrative's main character to embellish and frame the retelling and thus emphasize certain characteristics.

Verbalizing is an act of memory in and of itself. In talking about one's ancestors, community, and family, one is performing an act of memorization, reconstruction, and representation. Within a community, such re-presentation occurs continually, but to be effective, for the narrator to attain the status that he or she desires, the retelling of narratives must be done responsibly and with accountability. If narratives are treated irresponsibly, the listening community may draw very different conclusions about the narrator and the narrative performance will come to naught.

Symbolic representations of ancestors within the drama of the *famadihana* ceremonies, as when the ancestors vicariously enjoy a cere-

Fig. 11. Once re-enshrouded, the ancestors are lifted onto the shoulders of the waiting family members who dance vigorously with them (1993).

monial meal and then proclaim their thanks through the actions of the invited guests, contribute to the memory process as well. By actually performing the ancestors' actions, thereby creating a form of body memory, the ancestors become increasingly real and tangible for the living. Moreover, the physicality of some narratives is equally important and can underscore the serious nature of the ancestor-descendant relationships. There is a close relationship between the physical nature of an activity or an object and the physical nature of a memory. When understood as process, in that it is performed repeatedly, an activity such as weaving creates a physical or bodily memory in which one's body remembers the specific actions constituting the activity, which in turn creates and enhances the mental image of memory. The physicality of an object such as a burial shroud is similarly mnemonic.

Interpersonal relationships can also be a combination of verbal and non-verbal interaction. Public proclamations, which are often accompanied by presentations of tangible gifts, are powerful mechanisms for manipulating public opinion and establishing one's relationship to others, and thus one's identity. It was with great interest that I watched as my identity in highland Madagascar changed through public proclamations during ancestral events. Ancestral narratives are similarly public proclamations, but of memories that are verbalized and thus made real.

Memory is highly political in that it is a medium for establishing relationships and contextual narratives and for identity formation. James Clifford points to "the whole question of identity as [based on] a politics rather than an inheritance" (Clifford 1992, qtd. in Ong 1995, 351). As a politically charged medium, retelling memories is not a simple chronological recounting of all that transpired, but is the result of a very specific, agenda-based series of choices made by the teller, who manipulates the raw material to create a narrative to serve his or her own purpose. To this end, what is left unsaid is as important as that said. Forgetting or leaving out is just as important since "forgetting can be . . . an intentional and purposive attempt to create absences that can be crucial to the reconstruction and revaluation of social meanings and relations" (Weiss 1996, 133).

To conclude, I would like to point out that just as my Malagasy friends and family use ancestral memories to represent or re-present themselves for the consumption of others, this chapter is a form of mediated representation. It is a result of my own memories of my experiences while living in highland Madagascar, used and selected to make points or provide examples that work for my agenda of writing a chapter for inclusion in this book.

Notes

1. Funerary practices in Madagascar's central highlands incorporate rich and vibrant visual and performative art traditions. As an Africanist art historian, I became interested in Madagascar and funerary practices in the late 1980s. I traveled to Madagascar three times between 1990 and 1997, staying for a total of more than two years, with the help of a Social Science Research Council Pre-dissertation Fellowship, a Fulbright-Hays Doctoral Dissertation Research Grant, and an Indiana University Women's Studies Program Grant. I studied and participated in numerous ancestral ceremonies and spoke with youths, elders, diviners, shroud weavers, shroud vendors, friends, neighbors, acquaintances, and strangers—anyone who would take the time to talk with me—about highland Malagasy art and culture, particularly as they relate to the intricate and sophisticated ancestral traditions, and especially to funerary practices.

2. Justine Razanamanana (personal communication, 1992).

3. See also Bourdieu's discussion on repetition, or *habitus* (1986, 78).

4. Silk, either indigenous (*landibe*) or more recently imported mulberry (*landikely*) is considered *the* appropriate material, although economic hardship often causes families to provide shrouds made of cotton or nylon.

5. Decary (1962, 79). Presumably the epidemic ended once this ceremony was enacted and the ancestor was appeased.

6. Solange Razaka (personal communication, 1990) related this series of dreams experienced by her grandmother.

7. Mr. Ramomonjisoa, a *mpanandro* (diviner), from Manankasina Arivonimamo (personal communication, 1993).

8. Helinirina Ravoniarisoa, a *lambamena* (burial shroud) vendor in Arivonimamo, related this narrative about her mother (personal communication, 1993). The extreme verbal abuse in calling her a bitch mirrors the label "dog" given to an ancestor who does not receive a shroud, or receives one of such poor quality that it will disintegrate before the next *famadihana,* when it can be replaced. Moreover, tombs can only be opened once a year, and special permission must be secured from local authorities to open it a second time within the year.

9. Ratsizafy and his son Pano Ravelomparivo (personal communication, 1992).

10. After I moved to the Betsileo town of Sandrandahy, I watched my relationship to the townspeople develop and change, as it was described and categorized by my friends and colleagues there. Individuals are publicly acknowledged during ceremonial events as announcers loudly proclaim each attendee's name and geographic identity (tomb location or home town) while presenting gifts of beef corresponding to the amount of the original attendee's

gift to the family. During such events, my name changed from the *vazaha* (foreigner) from *andafy* (abroad), to Rebek from Sandrandahy. In this way, I witnessed my incorporation into the community as the community elders and spokespeople claimed me as their own. As my relationships and friendships deepened, I was honored to ultimately be adopted into a Betsileo family. I was given a fictive position as the sister of Bako Ramiliarisoa, and simultaneously entered into a joking relationship with her husband, Jean-René Rason, being referred to jokingly as his "second wife." Everyone in town knew me as part of this family, and accorded me the rights associated with this role and expected the accompanying responsibilities of me. Thus I was invited to ancestral events as a member of my Betsileo family, and was expected to participate in activities as well as obligations (helping with food and serving, dancing, dressing with and like my family, singing, sitting with the dead, and making payments to host families).

11. The act of blessing someone is called *tso-drano,* which means "to blow water," and usually involves splashing water or blowing (spritzing) water from one's mouth over the recipient's head.

12. According to Grandidier, the Merina woman's remains were continually transferred between the tombs of her two husbands. Eventually, one husband's second wife died and was buried in his tomb, which then decided the final resting place for the first wife as being in the tomb belonging to her other husband.

13. I heard this story a number of times while living in Arivonimamo in 1992-93, including from weavers Mme. Razafindrahova and M. Ranaivozandry.

14. *Tolam-balo* comes from "*tolana*" or bones, and "*valo*" or eight. Thus, the fundamental essence of a person's soul is said to rest in their "eight bones," the symbolic numerical and physical embodiment of the dry corpse.

Works Cited

Babcock, Barbara A. 1995. "'Not in the Absolute Singular': Rereading Ruth Benedict." *Women Writing Culture.* Ed. Ruth Behar and Deborah A. Gordon. London: U of California P. 104-30.

Bourdieu, Pierre. 1986. *Outline of a Theory of Practice.* Cambridge: Cambridge UP.

Briggs, Charles L. 1986. *Learning How to Ask: A Sociolinguistic Appraisal of the Role of the Interview in Social Science Research.* New York: Cambridge UP.

Carrithers, Michael. 1990. "Why Humans Have Cultures." *Man* 25.2: 189-206.

Clifford, James. 1992. "Traveling Cultures." *Cultural Studies.* Ed. Lawrence Grossberg, Cary Nelson, and Paula A. Treichler. New York: Routledge.

D'Azevedo, Warren. 1973. *The Traditional Artist in African Societies.* Bloomington, IN: Indiana UP.

Decary, Raymond. 1962. *La Mort et les Couturnes Funéraires à Madagascar.* Paris: G. P. Maisonneuve et Larose.

Drewal, Henry John. 1984. "Art, History, and the Individual: A New Perspective for the Study of African Visual Traditions." *Iowa Studies in African Art* 1: 87-101.

Drewal, Margaret Thompson. 1992. *Yoruba Ritual: Performers, Play, Agency.* Bloomington: Indiana UP.

Giddens, Anthony. 1976. "Production and Reproduction of Social Life." *New Rules of Sociological Method: A Positive Critique of Interpretive Sociologies.* New York: Basic.

Graeber, David. 1995. "Dancing with Corpses Reconsidered: An Interpretation of Famadihana (in Arivonimamo, Madagascar)." *American Ethnologist* 22.2: 258-78.

Grandidier, Guillaume. 1891. "Funeral Ceremonies among the Malagasy." *Antananarivo Annual and Madagascar Magazine* 4.15: 304-18.

Green, Rebecca L. 1996. "Addressing and Redressing the Ancestors: Weaving, the Ancestors, and Reburials in Highland Madagascar." Ph.D. dissertation, Indiana U.

——. 1998. *Once Is Never Enough: Ancestors, Reburials, and Weaving in Highland Madagascar.* Bloomington, IN: Indiana U Art Museum.

Karp, Ivan. 1986. "Agency and Social Theory: A Review of Anthony Giddens." *American Ethnologist* 13.1: 131-37.

Kondo, Dorinne. 1995. "Bad Girls: Theater, Women of Color, and the Politics of Representation." *Women Writing Culture.* Ed. Ruth Behar and Deborah A. Gordon. Berkeley: U of California P. 49-64.

McNaughton, Patrick R. 1988. *The Mande Blacksmiths: Knowledge, Power, and Art in West Africa.* Bloomington, IN: Indiana UP.

Ong, Aihwa. 1995. "Women Out of China: Traveling Tales and Traveling Theories in Postcolonial Feminism." *Women Writing Culture.* Ed. Ruth Behar and Deborah A. Gordon. Berkeley: U of California P. 350-72.

Royce, Anya Peterson. 1982. *Ethnic Identity: Strategies of Diversity.* Bloomington, IN: Indiana UP.

Ruud, Jorgen. 1960. *Taboo: A Study of Malagasy Customs and Belief.* Oslo: Oslo UP.

Schechner, Richard. 1986. Preface. Turner 7-20.

Turner, Victor. 1986. *The Anthropology of Performance.* New York: PAJ.

Weiss, Brad. 1996. "Dressing at Death: Clothing, Time, and Memory in Buhaya, Tanzania." *Clothing and Difference: Embodied Identities in Colonial and Post-Colonial Africa.* Ed. Hildi Hendrickson. Durham: Duke UP. 133-54.

2

DEATH AND REMEMBRANCE:
ADDRESSING THE COSTS OF LEARNING ANATOMY
THROUGH THE MEMORIALIZATION OF DONORS

Kathleen Dixon

This chapter examines relationships that can be established between students' experiences in the Gross Anatomy laboratory and the practice of memorializing individuals who donate their bodies for medical education. A brief description of laboratory work sets the stage for discussions of the development and significance of formal donor memorialization. Two central experiences of Gross Anatomy, *personalization* and *identification,* are described. *Personalization* refers to the cadaver's ability to evoke the personhood of the deceased and students' consequent speculations about the donor's identity and history. *Identification* refers to experiences in which students' own vulnerabilities are projected onto or exchanged with the cadaver's. This chapter assesses the potential of donor memorial services to answer questions associated with personalization and identification. Careful attention is given to the ways those responses influence the moral and professional development of medical students.

The Plight of the Anatomy Student
To enter the Gross Anatomy laboratory is to cross a threshold that connects and separates worlds.[1] In the room, there are rows of gleaming metal tables. Dozens of cadavers command one's view. When they are covered, the image is a stark presentation of casualties. Death appears not yet in its particularities but in its universality, as our shared fate.
Students' experiences here are unique and jarring. As F. Gonzalez-Crussi (1995) writes, their task is "squarely to confront the dead and, violating their most intimate individuality, to collect the information

with which truthful, testable abstractions may be built" (65-66). Under bright lights, sharp instruments pry open the body, forcing it to reveal its secrets. The quick are challenged not only by the sights but the scents of the dead. Parts of the body awaiting later dissection are wrapped in cloths soaked in formaldehyde. This produces a pungent odor that lingers in the nostrils and clings to clothing and books. Cadavers themselves, if improperly prepared, begin to deteriorate and produce strong, offensive odors (Hafferty 1991, 146).

In the Gross Anatomy laboratory the dead are dismembered in the name of medical education.[2] The force and implications of these encounters are disturbing. As one student put it, "We were doing something that would be a crime in our society if we weren't medical students, and that kind of violation of someone's body and privacy, that's significant" (Scott Russell, qtd. in Schoenberg 1991, 27). The brutality of anatomization can be redeemed by the educational value of the material displayed. Thus, instructors' prosections[3] are seen as both elegant and highly functional. However, students' cadavers rarely reflect this ideal and instead offer mute testimony to the price of education. Bisected and torn tissues seem to reproach students for their lack of technical expertise. Stephen Hoffman (1986), reflecting on his experiences in Gross Anatomy lab, recalled,

We also experienced a twinge of sadness when we gazed upon our work. It was clear that we were abusing what used to be the substance of a person. What we snipped at cavalierly and pried recklessly apart was once the sacred province of a life. All of us, I think, felt a growing sense of guilt as the semester went on. (11)

Robin Graf said, "I guess there's no graceful way of dissecting, but it seems so . . . vulgar sometimes, that you're actually doing this to a human being" (qtd. in Schoenberg 1991, 27). Because human remains are encountered as human beings, dissection becomes desecration without the warrant provided by a donor's knowledgeable consent. One student observed, "It makes dissecting a lot easier if you believe that your guy had donated his body . . . given permission for you to do all of this" (Hafferty 1991, 83).[4]

In the Gross Anatomy laboratory, death assumes the role of teacher. While students may seek relief in abstraction and technical detail, particular encounters refocus their attention on the fact and significance of death. Confrontations with universal mortality are sufficiently challenging. However, moments when death is individualized can shape or threaten values and identities. One is forced to face the implications of the irrevocable loss of unique personhood. Even a glimpse of this can be distressing. The one whose exploration of the viscera was unproblematic may be brought up short by the sight of pink fingernail polish on a cadaver's hands (Schoenberg 1991, 27). However, students can also appreciate the personal and professional implications of these lessons in mortality:

A lot of people around here think they will see enough of death sooner or later, so they figure they don't have to worry or think about it now. These people don't react, they just cope and that's just sandbagging. Even if it works in the short run, you're just stealing from Paul to pay Peter. Sooner or later you'll have to pay the price—if not in your inability to deal with your patients' needs as they lay dying, then certainly in your own inability to deal with your own death and even paradoxically in the inability of others to care for you at that time. Sooner or later it all comes home. (Hafferty 1991, 119)

Healing through Memorialization

Some institutions, recognizing the painful and challenging nature of the experiences of the Gross Anatomy laboratory, have chosen to confront these issues directly. In 1980, Wright State University's School of Medicine held one of the first memorial services for those who donated their bodies to the institution for medical education and research (Schoenberg 1991, 27). In 1986, the Medical College of Virginia held the first of its annual services to commemorate its donors (MacPherson 1990, 9). Medical schools at Tulane University, the University of Massachusetts at Worcester, and West Virginia University are also among those that conduct donor memorial services (MacPherson 1990, 9).

In 1990, students at the Medical College of Ohio (MCO) developed the first of what would become annual Anatomy Memorial Services. They recognized the importance of taking time to remember and honor those who donated their bodies to the college for the advancement of medical education and science. But the ceremony also expresses awareness of the human costs of gaining understanding and expertise in the health sciences.

The experiences grounding this chapter began with an invitation to speak at MCO's Anatomy Memorial Service. I felt both humbled and uplifted by the emotional power and integrity of the service. Students' genuine gratitude and concern for donors and their families made a deep impression upon me. This service establishes connections between people who might not otherwise meet. Family members and loved ones of donors are introduced to students. Feelings of shared purpose and community are elicited through music, poetry, and prayer.

When students reveal their appreciation of the donors' and loved ones' sacrifices, when they respectfully acknowledge the dignity of the gift and giver, families' anxieties regarding donation or use of the cadaver are relieved. At the first MCO Anatomy Memorial Service, after students completed a ceremony in which a candle was lit for each donor, one family member whispered to another, "Now I know why he did it" (Schoenberg 1991, 27). Families' willingness to open personal journals and albums, to share publicly the rich identity and history of their loved ones, brings closure to students' questions and speculations. When families speak with them and articulate the personal commitments that led to donation, students can begin to see this gift as an expression of important values and beliefs. This can relieve some of the burdens of guilt or grief that students may have carried.

Anatomy Lessons: Echoes of a Life

The invasive encounter with anonymous human remains is one of the most difficult aspects of Gross Anatomy for students. Donors' bodies powerfully evoke their presence and personhood. Of one hundred first-year students queried at "City Medical School," only nine indicated they had never "thought about who their cadaver had been in life" (Hafferty 1991, 82). Students often characterize the cadaver as a "formerly living human being," conveying their recognition of its unique identity and history (Hafferty 1991, 99-102, 106-8). We might meaningfully speak then of students' experiences of *personalization* of cadavers. Experiences of personalization prompt speculations about the donor's identity, history, or mode of death. They may also induce reflection on the decision to donate. How did the donor view processes of anatomization? What beliefs or social contexts induced this person to make such a gift?

Personalization is not an easy experience. It can be emotionally taxing or even wrenching. This may account for some of the sleep disturbances, nightmares, and altered perceptions experienced by students. Frederick W. Hafferty (1991) indicates that roughly 20 percent of "City" students acknowledged having such experiences during the first few weeks of lab (94). These experiences may continue or resurface during particularly difficult points of dissection. Hafferty argues, "The most emotionally disquieting periods of dissection for students were the head, face, and arm prosections, and the neck, pelvic, and perineal dissections. Thoughts of the cadaver as a formerly living human being were inexorably and often unexpectedly heightened by anatomy exercises focusing on these regions" (1991, 90). Even long-term inhabitants of the laboratory are not immune to these effects. One lab instructor reported, "About twice a year I have the same dream, always the same one. The cadaver that I'm working on sits up, very angry with me for what I am doing to him" (Hafferty 1991, 136).

Given the intrusive and violent nature of the students' tasks, they need to organize their work in ways that defuse painful emotions and legitimate dissection. Students often acknowledge the comparative ease of objectification and the immediate instrumental gains associated with refusal to personalize the cadaver. As one student explained,

There's no way I can think of my cadaver as having lived. If I do that, all I do is go to pieces. Every day before I go into lab, I have to gear myself up by thinking about muscles and anatomical structures so that when I actually get into lab there would be no way that I could think of it as human. I know it's a protective device, but I couldn't do it any other way. (Hafferty 1991, 102)

Some students contrast personalization with the preferred professional demeanor of cool detachment or "scientific" neutrality. A "City" medical student explained:

I just ignore [the humanity of] my cadaver. . . . We're not supposed to react to that. To me a cadaver is a scary plastic . . . [entity]. If the reality ever hits that this is human, then it's going to be really bad. If you think every human being will look like that when he dies, you'll go crazy. Most medical students resort to the intellectual microcosm . . . once they get working. At first I didn't agree with this perspective, but now I see it is the only way to function. (Hafferty 1991, 103)

Traditional responses to human dissection have emphasized the need for emotional distance and abstraction. The famed eighteenth-century anatomist, William Hunter, braced his students, warning them: "Anatomy is the Basis of Surgery, it informs the Head, guides the hand, and familiarizes the heart to a kind of necessary Inhumanity" (qtd. in Iserson 1994, 91). This legacy is encapsulated in one contemporary student's assertion: "We're there to memorize not philosophize" (Hafferty 1991, 104). Unfortunately, students may refuse to discuss their experiences for fear of violating tacit professional rules prohibiting emotional disclosure. They may hesitate to bring upon themselves the censure of lab mates or instructors (Hafferty 1991, 84). One student stated,

No one seemed to have a big problem, but then, nobody is talking about it either so I really wouldn't know. Maybe conversations about how one feels about lab are taboo. I guess it's not something to talk about. If you're sick about it, you don't want others to know. I get the impression that I'm the only one feeling these things. . . . Others look down on you and say you're not fit to be a doctor. (Hafferty 1991, 127)

This leaves students little space in which to conduct important philosophical or emotional work. Isolation also exacerbates their feelings of deviancy. As one student said,

The worst thing about lab is thinking that you're alone—alone in your reactions, in how you feel about lab. If you could talk to other people about how you are feeling and maybe find out that they are feeling the same things, that would be the biggest help right there. (Hafferty 1991, 127)

Experiences of personalization need not be unduly painful or traumatizing. Students often acknowledge the personal and professional gains associated with reflection on themes of death and dying. One student observed:

Working with the cadaver was the best thing that ever happened to me as far as helping me get started in the direction of dealing with my fears and anxieties about death. Lab shocked and upset me, and that was good. I wanted to be shocked out of my stable, complacent, philosophically detached attitudes about death. Just seeing dead bodies, looking at their faces, drove home the point that I would die someday, too. It was like looking death in the face and realizing that I would look like that and become just an object. It drove home the point that this was the natural order of things. I don't have all the answers I need, but at least I've started thinking about them. (Hafferty 1991, 120)

Some students argue that this kind of philosophical reflection is one of the most important experiences of Gross Anatomy lab (Hafferty 1991, 119).

The cadaver also affords students the opportunity to model empathic responses that should characterize their later interactions with patients (Hafferty 1991, 101). Willingness to explicitly work through issues of personalization becomes a sign of intellectual flexibility, candor, and emotional availability which are expected to benefit future patients. These benefits are seen as justifying this openness even when it subjects students to acute distress:

It's a really easy thing to do, to become too insensitive and hardened in lab. I've seen it happen to a lot of people. . . . [They] just go about their business, ready to cut anything. Part of their coolness is an insensitivity to other people. . . . That type of thing is what I want to fight against. It can be really easy to carry over the insensitivity you acquire in lab to other things. (Hafferty 1991, 107)

How might empathic consideration of the cadaver be linked with humane response to the suffering of living patients? Although it is speculative, we might seek analogies in treatment settings in which patients are unconscious or noncommunicative. Robert Zussman (1992) describes young physicians' responses to patients treated in two intensive care units. Residents lament being surrounded by death. They discuss the difficulties created by the lack of interaction with patients. One resident explained, "Sometimes you walk through there and you feel like you're part of a large science experiment on humans because all these things are going on. . . . So it's a very hard place to work . . . it's so stressful and so relatively unsatisfying" (52). In these ICUs, residents often fail to recognize the patient who is nearly buried beneath layers of devices and treat their data instead (Zussman 1992, 58-59). For these physicians, the process of obtaining a diagnosis or formulating effective therapy becomes an intellectual puzzle or "physiology experiment" (Zussman 1992, 59). This game can become an end in itself. One resident observed,

I don't know how much of it [treatment] was done because they actually thought they could bring this person back to [being] a viable human being more than we got him to live during his stay in the ICU. In a competitive place where these people pride themselves on being such good doctors, that idea is sometimes prevalent. (Zussman 1992, 59)

Perhaps the process of personalization with its empathic connections with another's identity, history, and values could prevent interventions which physicians see as tortuous and which result in high levels of provider guilt and stress. Whether in the ICU or the Gross Anatomy laboratory, practitioners struggle to reconstruct the other's identity in ways that help them to establish both moral constraints and goals for their work.

Some practices in the Gross Anatomy laboratory facilitate depersonalization. As in surgery, the use of drapes transforms human bodies into something else: appropriate workspaces. This process of abstraction provides students some measure of relief. Kenneth Iserson (1994) describes students' initial encounters with their cadavers in the lab:

The cadavers are laid out on individual metal tables which the medical students approach, usually very hesitantly, in groups of four—two on each side. Each pair is assigned to dissect one side of the cadaver. The students first cover the head, hands and feet with formaldehyde-soaked cloths and plastic bags to better preserve them for later dissection. This also serves the purpose of partially depersonalizing the corpse, since the body is now (temporarily) faceless. Since many of these students have never even seen a corpse outside of a funeral home, this can be a traumatic experience.

With this procedure behind them, the students turn their cadavers face-down and begin the dissection of the back muscles. Beginning the dissection here serves two purposes. The back is one of the least personal parts of the body and so is the least psychologically threatening to the students. And since these budding physicians have rarely, if ever, held a scalpel (correctly) to cut on human flesh, they can do the least amount of damage to important anatomical structures on the broad expanse of the back. (93-94)

Humor is another conventional strategy for dealing with the emotional and psychological stresses associated with dissection. Freud argued that "humor is a sort of defense mechanism that allows people to face a difficult situation without becoming overwhelmed with unpleasant emotions."[5] Others have emphasized the role of humor as a "potential moderator or minimizer of serious or adverse life events" (Hall and Rappe 1995, 290). One form of humor recognizes and deflates anxieties associated with traces of the deceased person. Frederick Hafferty (1991) analyzes students' practices of giving cadavers humorous names in order to depersonalize them and reduce the threats associated with their dissection. The disturbingly present but unknown "individual" becomes Abber Cadaver, Anne Nomaly, or Kay Daver (Hafferty 1991, 85).

Although humor provides temporary relief and distraction that may prevent sensory, emotional, or psychological overload, helping students to complete the immediate task at hand (Hall and Rappe 1995, 291), it may not adequately address the larger issues of personal mortality and loss raised by the cadaver. Death is quietly persistent. In a moment, their defenses are breached and students acknowledge the loss of this specific and unique individual. Stephen Hoffman (1986) describes the experience quite powerfully:

Once we began the abdominal dissection, we discovered that our cadaver was flawed. I remember opening the abdomen for the first time with a clean midline slit. Looking unsuspectingly within, we saw a body riddled with tumors. Our group fell silent. We were saddened. Somehow this encounter had taken us beyond the realm of the abstract. Suddenly our body had become personified. From the telltale appearance of his insides, we could tell something about the quality of our man's last days and about the way he had probably died. Our cadaver had become exempted from anonymity. (11-12)

Shared vulnerability links students inextricably with the deceased as they face the reality of their own deaths. Instances of rehumanization of cadavers, even those that heighten issues of identification, although poignant and painful experiences, need not be injurious. Students may establish connections with those now deceased. They can reflect on human fragility and our common need for care and protection. Iserson describes his own experience:

The power of this type of personalization was brought home to me as a medical student when one dissection group was told that their cadaver had been a physician and another group was told that the young body (our age) they were dissecting was that of a leukemia victim who had been a premedical student before becoming ill. We then really understood that each of these bodies had a human history. (1994, 96)

At Last We Meet: The Effects of Remembrance

Memorial services can enhance processes of personalization. Students cannot help but speculate about the identity and origins of their cadavers, searching the bodies for traces of the deceased's interests and experiences. To do so is to recognize shared humanity. Students have so many questions: "Whose body is this?" "What did she do?" "What works and loves engaged his mind, heart, and hands?" Why not answer these questions directly?

Some memorial services fail to resolve these mysteries and preserve the anonymity of donors.[6] But at MCO a more powerful sense of the presence of donors is evoked through photographs projected before those assembled. The images, which are selected by families, allow students to see the donors through their loved ones' eyes. Those at the medical school move shyly and perhaps even with a sense of awe into a family's circle of intimacy. Candid photographs capture a prankster's hijinks, stop students' breath with the strength of loving embraces, and allow families to delight in scampering children. More carefully choreographed images celebrate tremendous achievements and the pride of family. The answers to important questions are revealed as donors' names are read aloud, explicitly connecting the bodies students encountered with persons' visual histories.

Although I felt the effectiveness of this choice during the ceremony, it has taken some time to develop a deeper appreciation of its moral strength. These proceedings foster awareness of personal sacrifices and produce a commitment that generic or class-based expressions of gratitude rarely match. Students identify their benefactors and acknowledge their debts. The donor's past is connected to the student's professional future. This, I believe, can deepen the student's sense of commitment to others.

This individual connection established through the memorial service also produces an interesting legacy for families. The donors were and will continue to be these medical students' teachers, for they made a sacred contribution to the development of these students' professional skills. If students carry part of their teachers' commitments forward with them in their own work, donors enjoy an important form of social endurance. Families can be comforted by the knowledge that when these students are fully fledged, their skill and compassion will offer testimony to their loved one. It's a plausible form of immortality.

Perhaps families can even enjoy the whispered presence of the loved one when they receive medical care. Margaret Stroebe and others (1995) offer a compelling critique of models of grief and mourning that require individuals to achieve the social extinction of the deceased. They draw on historical models and contemporary cases to argue that survivors instead renegotiate the terms and nature of their relationships with the deceased. The bereaved sustain the deceased in part through their commitment to her values and ideas. They enjoy a sense of muted connection with their loved one through this nexus. Because the donor's gift links the family and the medical profession, bereaved families could be uplifted by the loved one's gift whenever they receive medical care.

What other benefits for medical students can be furthered in this type of memorial service? I believe this experience can facilitate and reinforce the shift from simple recognition of someone's pain to the morally profound understanding of another person's *suffering*. Hoffman (1986) suggests this in his description of the silence and sense of tragedy evoked when he opened the cadaver's abdomen and saw a body filled with tumors. It was not just an encounter with the traces of pain that stopped the students. They met the man by recognizing his suffering.

Eric Cassell (1991) argues, "Suffering occurs when an impending destruction of the person is perceived; it continues until the threat of disintegration has passed or until the integrity of the person can be restored in some other manner" (33). To recognize and address suffering is to connect ourselves with the identities, interests, and welfare of unique persons. Hoffman allowed the tumors to evoke a sense of the man's suffering. He and his colleagues began to understand "the quality of our man's last days and . . . the way he had probably died" (1986, 12). This understanding can be much stronger and clearer when students are given glimpses into pictorial histories, read notes from biographies, and hear stories that helped to shape a person's life. I suspect that some of the muffled sobs I heard from students during the ceremony were the result of these sudden and vivid connections. Much of what illness threatened and subsequently destroyed was revealed to them. No wonder they wept.

Yet, if students find this meeting with the persons their anatomy cadavers once were painful or sorrowful, should it be encouraged? Cassell puts the matter in sharp perspective, stating:

Withdrawal from the patient is rewarded with certainty and punished by sterile inadequate knowledge; movement toward the patient is rewarded with knowledge and punished with uncertainties. The fact remains, however, that to disengage from the patient is to lose the ultimate source of knowledge in medicine. (1991, 232)

Cassell contends that healing is accomplished by means of a relationship between the doctor and the unique person whose suffering she appreciates. If he is correct, recognition of the person the cadaver once was and of the sources and significance of his suffering is the first step on the road to becoming a healer (Cassell 1991, 234).

My Body, My Self

The decision to face squarely the challenges presented by the donor's gift and the significance of his suffering and death may shape the maturing identity and values of the medical student. There is, however, another important but yet unaddressed aspect of experiences in the Gross Anatomy laboratory. Juan de Valverde introduced remarkable anatomical engravings in his *Anatomia del corpo umano* (1560).[7] Valverde's images are striking in that they both present and deflect recognition of the violence of the anatomists' art. Rather than cadavers—bodies that may have been stolen and exhibited, whose anatomization would be seen as mutilation—we see *donors*—people who offer themselves and demonstrate their own features to the eye of the anatomist. The voluntary nature of the gift and its sacrifices are presented clearly as body parts and organ systems as a man lifts his own omentum to bare his viscera to our view (Laqueur 1990, 76).

However, the most striking and perhaps enigmatic of Valverde's engravings shows an anatomist, himself dissected and open to view, his fingers resecting the ribs of a cadaver that I consider *his other self, his twin* (Laqueur 1990, 77). The anatomist's face is presented in profile; he does not look at his work, but is arrested in thought, gazing at something not in our field of view. His expression is somber, his eyes uplifted. The engraving also contains two images of the heart. Perhaps this is the heart of the anatomist, revealed in his studies? These images are shocking. However, they reveal an important experience of anatomists working with human cadavers: identification. Identification refers to experiences in which the dissector's own vulnerabilities are projected onto or exchanged with the cadaver's. Identification can also take the direct and explicit form of imaginary substitutions of self for the cadaverous donor. Hafferty expressed this in his response to the first day of Gross Anatomy laboratory at "City Medical School." As he left the laboratory, detached composure slipped away and he realized, "Somewhere among those forty-four bodies I had seen my own face" (1991, 81).

I believe anatomists have always expected to encounter themselves upon the anatomy table. This suspicion or latent realization is a source of dread as students and professionals approach cadavers. Hafferty indicates that anatomy students see donors' corpses as "self-referents." As one student explained, "You've got to remember that in a way, that's you lying there, and come to grips with that fact. It's not the easiest thing in the world to do" (Hafferty 1991, 99, 119). Students' nightmares reflect these difficulties, featuring terrifying scenes in which they become a cadaver (Hafferty 1991, 94).

Identification can heighten the sense of desecration and trauma associated with dissection. Injury is not only internalized, but can be articulated in ways suggestive of retributive balance. If the shadow of justice is visible in these troubling perceptions, one might anticipate experiences of heightened anxiety and resistance to donating their own bodies among students enrolled in Gross Anatomy. Hafferty discovered that "most of the students at City were vehemently opposed to the idea of donating their own bodies to a medical school to be used as cadavers" (1991, 84). Students' arguments against donating their bodies emphasized the violence, dehumanization, and loss of dignity they associated with dissection. One student exclaimed, "Oh, no! I don't want anybody hacking me up and throwing the pieces around. . . . Who even wants to think that that's what you're going to become" (Hafferty 1991, 123). Another said,

I used to think that I would [donate my body], but not now. It's not rational, but it's just kind of degrading to think of yourself as a cadaver. Who wants first-year medical students to make jokes while they're pulling your lungs out? I just couldn't depersonalize my own body in that way. (Hafferty 1991, 123)

It's very interesting to note that "the more removed students are from lab (in time or space), the more willing they are to consider donating their bodies to be used as cadavers" (Hafferty 1991, 122). Does distance blunt the impact of identification?

Students may actually experience relief when they uncover parts of a cadaver whose features limit or block identification. A "City" medical student struggled to explain the experience:

It sounds kind of strange to put it in this way, but I felt relieved when I finally looked at the cadaver and especially his face because it was a total stranger. It didn't look like anybody I knew. Maybe even more than that was that the face didn't even look very human anyway. It wasn't very well preserved and part of the face had been all pressed in. That was good. I would have been a lot more upset if it had looked more human. (Hafferty 1991, 104)

Something this student dreaded had not come to pass. That cadaver could not carry portents of the student's own death. Its vulnerability and the violence of its dissection could be kept separate from his or her post-death fate. Further, the student's vulnerability to loss and grief could not be elicited by a face whose features were reminiscent of those of family or friends. Identification had not occurred. The student could relax, sighing, "This is not me."

And yet it is. Cadavers can remind students of an essential, shared humanity, the universal human being in vulnerability and death. If students looking down see themselves mirrored in the flesh of a corpse, they experience their own mortality. As one student observed, "Dissecting a cadaver makes it very real that you're going to die" (Hafferty 1991, 118). This realization can lead students to confront themselves. Perhaps Valverde's image doesn't express fears of retributive violence but suggests a positive personal transformation accomplished through penetrating reflection and analysis. Acknowledgments of mortality and vulnerability could facilitate processes of life-review. Students may be poised to ask, "Why am I here?" "Whom do I serve and why?" These are crucial questions. Their answers have to be sought with the heart as well as the mind. Thus, in the anatomy laboratory, through identification donors take students beyond what is normally visible in themselves and challenge them to pursue deeper questions.

If the experience of identification prompts students to probe their own beliefs, values, and commitments, MCO's Anatomy Memorial Service represents the opportunity to make and share a kind of progress report. The students who carefully plan these ceremonies, who present them as gifts to donors' families express *through them* their understanding of their own defining values and responsibilities. Planning meetings offer opportunities to test individual and collective assessments of the broader aspects of their education in Gross Anatomy. Intellectual growth or moral development can be reviewed and charted. This process facilitates important moments of self-definition. Students may say, "I am the one who met these challenges. These are the ways in which what I learned shaped who I am." If there is an element of rite of passage in the travails of Gross Anatomy, MCO's memorial service brings closure to this stage of the students' development. They may stand before the community, speak out their understandings and commitments and be recognized. It is especially poignant and promising that they choose to do so in ways that do not prioritize their own achievements, but instead celebrate others' identity and contributions.

The Anatomy Memorial Service may also function to break down barriers or resistance to identification. If the state of cadavers prohibited or complicated processes of identification, photographs of donors facilitate this connection. When students laugh at children's antics captured on film, when they see graduation, wedding, or reunion pictures of the donor, they readily identify with the persons donors were. Here is a family much like theirs. Life experiences they have had or anticipate are lovingly portrayed. It is a short distance to consideration of one's own cherished memories and mementos. It is a further, but nonetheless manageable walk to thoughts of one's own death. Personalized donor memorial services might prompt reflection on the ways in which students themselves would like to be remembered. This could lead to life-review and consideration of personal identity and values.

As we have seen, donor memorial services can advance resolution of issues of personalization and identification raised in Gross Anatomy lab. They establish important connections between individuals. These rites can allow students, donors, and their families to meet, recognizing common needs and bonds. Personal memorializations implicitly acknowledge the realities and costs of death. Students may develop a new and richer understanding of the suffering donors experienced. This in turn brings heightened awareness or responsivity to grief. Students' recognition and expressions of gratitude for donors' and families' sacrifices can solidify an emerging sense of professional responsibility. Their development of memorial services affords students the opportunity to consider the philosophical and moral challenges associated with Gross Anatomy. They can articulate their understanding of the meanings of life and death and reflect on their own mortality. Thus, in this forum for reflections on death and our obligations of remembrance, the dead complete their undertaking and bring some closure to this stage of the education of the living.

Notes

I would like to thank the anonymous reviewers for the *Journal of Clinical Ethics*. They read my work with care and offered helpful suggestions which substantially improved the quality of the paper. I would also like to recognize and thank my colleague, Dr. Donald Callen, for his review of drafts and helpful commentary.

1. Kenneth V. Iserson (1994) describes this transition, saying, "The anatomy lab . . . introduces medical students into medicine's guild. Dissecting a human body is a rite-of-passage that the rest of the world knows of, wonders at, and fears" (92). Frederick W. Hafferty (1991) provides evidentiary support of this claim and links it with students' own perceptions. "While enveloped by their training experiences, medical students are prone to characterize their training as a rite of passage. Some accounts depicted medical training as a gauntlet of trials, emotional as well as academic. Others emphasized the ceremonial and ritualistic nature of either the educational process or the students' responses to it" (187). Hafferty argues that the "basic-science years" could be interpreted as a liminal phase. In this stage,

[I]nitiates move more completely into a world marked by "uncommon sense" . . . ambiguity, and a release from what had once been normal interpretive constraints. Individuals are asked to reinterpret and construct reality in new ways—thus becoming, in Turner's construction, "liminal monsters," involved in a "time outside time" where factors of everyday social construction are subverted, distorted, and denormalized. (187)

Students at "City Medical School" confirmed that Gross Anatomy laboratory separated them from laypersons and other professionals. One observed, "Anatomy is *the* subject that says you're in medical school" (Hafferty 1991, 53). Another student explained:

The cadaver represents a unique figure in your life. . . . It's impressive, so that when you talk to other people about it they are taken aback. They can't understand how you can do it. Having done it, it sets you apart. It's one of the biggest symbols of medical school. It distinguishes us as medical students unlike a course in biochemistry could ever do. Anatomy is the one thing that medical students do that other people don't. (Hafferty 1991, 53)

"City" medical students also recognized Gross Anatomy as a testing or proving ground for their ability to identify and either implement or constructively modify "feelings rules" associated with the professional culture of medicine (Hafferty 1991, 14-18, 66-67, 188-90).

2. It is interesting to note that students themselves often remain unconvinced of the educational value of their human dissections. Hafferty describes high rates of absenteeism at "City's" Gross Anatomy laboratory: "Aside from peaks in attendance during prosections and thorax dissections, attendance dropped rapidly and consistently over the initial month of lab to about 50 percent and then, over the next two months, continued to decline less rapidly until the end of lab" (1991, 44). Students at "City" were not required to attend lab

and offered a variety of explanations for their absences. These included "in order of frequency, (1) the quality of the cadavers, (2) the quality of the lab instructors, and (3) labmate relations" (Hafferty 1991, 145). Students also believed that attendance in lab and participation in dissection were unnecessary as "City" had no practical, lab-based exams and dissection did not affect their performance on the multiple-choice exams which determined their grades in the course (Hafferty 1991, 145).

3. Hafferty defines this term,

Prosections are anatomical parts that have been previously dissected, often by faculty members, for use as teaching tools (for example, one arm dissected to show muscle and tendon structure, another to highlight the vascular system), thereby allowing students to view, in context, structures they might well destroy if they were allowed to attempt identification by dissecting on their own. (1991, 90)

4. Hafferty also records students' worries about the adequacy of donors' understanding of the processes of medical dissection. If donors "really had no idea what was going to happen," the moral value of their consent was impeached (1991, 84).

5. Sigmund Freud, "Humor," *International Journal of Psychoanalysis* 9 (1928): 1-6, qtd. in Hall and Rappe 1995, 290.

6. Describing the ceremonies at the Medical College of Virginia, MacPherson writes, "Never were the cadavers' named mentioned, though they are recorded in a register at the cemetery office. There was no reference to the ways the donors had lived and died, or to the reasons for the gift they had made." Donors' contributions and sacrifices are simply recognized en masse (1990, 9).

7. These images are reproduced and an interesting critical discussion can be found in Laqueur 1990, 76-77.

Works Cited

Cassell, Eric J. 1991. *The Nature of Suffering and the Goals of Medicine*. New York: Oxford UP.

DeSpelder, Lynn Ann, and Albert Lee Strickland, eds. 1995. *The Path Ahead: Readings in Death and Dying*. Mountain View, CA: Mayfield.

Gonzalez-Crussi, F. 1985. *Notes of an Anatomist*. San Diego: Harcourt, Brace, Jovanovich.

Hafferty, Frederick W. 1991. *Into the Valley: Death and the Socialization of Medical Students*. New Haven: Yale UP.

Hall, Mary N., and Paula T. Rappe. 1995. "Humor and Critical Incident Stress." DeSpelder and Strickland. 289-94.

Hoffman, Stephen A. 1986. *Under the Ether Dome: A Physician's Apprenticeship at Massachusetts General Hospital.* New York: Scribner's.

Iserson, Kenneth V. 1994. *Death to Dust: What Happens to Dead Bodies?* Tucson: Galen.

Laqueur, Thomas. 1990. *Making Sex: Body and Gender from the Greeks to Freud.* Cambridge: Harvard UP.

MacPherson, Peter. 1990. "Remembering the Donation: Memorial Service Honors Those Who Gave Their Bodies to Science." *American Medical News* 33 (9 Feb.): 9.

Schoenberg, Nara. 1991. "Anatomy of Compassion." *Toledo Blade* (2 Nov.): 27.

Stroebe, Margaret, Mary M. Gergen, Kenneth Gergen, and Wolfgang Stroebe. 1995. "Broken Hearts or Broken Bonds: Love and Death in Historical Perspective." DeSpelder and Strickland 230-41.

Zussman, Robert. 1992. *Intensive Care: Medical Ethics and the Medical Profession.* Chicago: U of Chicago P.

3

WOMEN ON DEATH ROW:
MEDIA REPRESENTATIONS OF FEMALE EVIL

Kathryn Ann Farr

The small population of women on death row in the United States provides a unique opportunity for examining representations of female evil. News stories on these women, who account for less than 2 percent of the total population of death row inmates, would seem to be a particularly rich source of such representations. Indeed, my own research showed that media portrayals of women on death row reflected prosecutorial claims that these women represented stereotypic forms of female evil. Featured in articles on these death-sentenced women were evil traits associated with femaleness, or with masculinized women. Representations included poisonous, seductive, and cold-hearted murderers of loved ones; sexual, young killers whose depravity matched that of their male crime partner; vengeful women with explosive personalities; and hardened drug addicts who, like men, murdered in the course of a robbery.

Presented here are findings from my study of newspaper and magazine articles on the thirty-five women on death row at the end of 1993, and their capital cases. The characterizations of them, I suggest, help preserve images of evil women that are culturally pervasive and entrenched. Such representations showcase female evil for which the most extreme controls are warranted.

Representations of Evil

While definitions of evil vary, they usually refer to intentional acts of destructiveness or harmfulness committed by a person or group. The individual evil-doer is often described as unrepentant, remorseless, and lacking empathy for those harmed, similar to the modern characterization of a sociopath or psychopath. Persons seen as engaging in evil acts may be depicted as inhuman, beastly, or of another species. Indeed, evil seems to be predicated on the existence, and thus an image, of an evil-doer. Positivist criminologists Caesare Lombroso and William Ferrero

(1895), for example, argued that the "born criminal" was a subhuman form suffering from atavistic moral degeneracy.

Contemporary sociologists and criminologists, however, have largely ignored the study of evil. Edwin Lemert (1997) has suggested that sociologists' "allegiance" to cultural relativism and their role as "unmaskers" of dubious moral claims make them reluctant to "apply terms like 'bad,' 'immoral,' or 'evil' except in descriptive or analytical contexts" (2). With its emphasis on norm violations and reactions to rule-breaking, deviance appears to be a less value-laden and more comfortable sociological concept.

Emile Durkheim (1938 [1915]), followed by a number of other early sociologists (e.g., Erikson 1966; Garfinkel 1956), described the functional role of deviance in setting forth moral boundaries and legitimating behaviors, attitudes, and values that maintain social cohesion. He further pointed out that "collective moral representations" are reaffirmed by punitive sanctions against the deviant. Additionally, deviance is functional in providing for the social control of illegitimate behaviors. Punishment can serve as both a specific and general deterrent, often strengthened by moral outrage.

Deviance scholars and social constructionists also have emphasized the importance of *representations* of evil. Some years ago, for example, Frank Tannenbaum (1994 [1938]) introduced the term "dramatization of evil" to describe the way in which juvenile play may be redefined as delinquent evil which must be suppressed. More recently, Craig Reinarman (1993) described strategies for dramatizing the drug problem that included "the *routinization of caricature*—rhetorically re-crafting worse cases into typical cases and the episodic into the epidemic" (96; emphasis in original).

As Tannenbaum says, the dramatization process often involves a "gradual shift from the definition of the specific acts as evil to a definition of the individual as evil, so that all his acts come to be looked upon with suspicion" (293)—resulting in what Erving Goffman (1963) describes as a "spoiled identity." Further, according to Tannenbaum, the assault must be made on the entire group (e.g., juvenile delinquents); that is, a whole category or class of people must be changed in order to suppress the "evil." The deviant stereotype is often linked to a population seen as threatening to the status quo, resulting in a stratified form of social control. From a social constructionist view, "categories are constructed and populations identified that confirm the reality of the deviation" (Farrell and Swigert 1988, 394). The discredited group, then, stands as its own best example.

Evil is also dramatized through initiation ceremonies or rituals in the process of becoming deviant (Erikson 1966; Becker 1963). In earlier times, public executions served this end (Lemert 1997). Today, media coverage of criminal trials ensures that initiation ceremonies are well publicized, that is, if the particular crime or criminal is deemed newsworthy.

Indeed, the media overplay violent and sexual crimes, leaving the false impression that such offenses constitute a large part of the crime problem in the United States (Ferrell and Sanders 1995; Sheley and Ashkins 1981). Joseph Sheley and Cindy Ashkins (1981) also report that, although society has become more diverse, media portrayals of criminals remain "homogenized," and include "distortions" relative to race, gender, and class. Media representations of offenders typically feature dangerous and frightening individuals, driven by inherent madness or immorality, a central element in the "marketing of moral outrage" (Ferrell and Sanders 1995, 31). Moral outrage is also fostered by media representation of the victim as innocent and vulnerable, or of suitably high social status.

Representations of Female Evil

Esther Madriz (1997) argues that theories emphasizing the importance of punishment and coercion in social control overlook the fact that "most of the mechanisms that control women's lives can be found in the codes, symbols, words, rituals, and images transmitted and reinforced almost daily by the mass media, films, stories" (31). Her point is well taken. Representations of evil women who go against norms of femininity, often harming or killing men and children, abound in early mythology and appear today in criminological work as well as popular culture.

Stereotypes of female evil are prominent in the criminological literature on female offenders from the late 1800s through the 1960s. Beginning in the late 1960s, feminist critiques challenged conventional assumptions about women and crime while pointing to their continuing influence on criminal justice decisions (Daly and Chesney-Lind 1988; Naffeine 1987; Carlen and Worrall 1985; Leonard 1982; Smart 1976; Simon 1975; Klein 1973; Heidensohn 1968).

One set of stereotypes features traits thought to be natural but undesirable in women, the flip side of their inherently benign nature. For example, the belief that women are cunning and manipulative explained women's tendency to commit crimes of deceit, lure men into crime, and keep their own criminal activity hidden from the law (Sparrow 1970; deRham 1969; Pollak 1950; Thomas 1923; Lombroso and Ferrero 1895; Pike 1876). A related theme is that female offenders are sexually wanton, often using their sexuality to seduce, exploit, and harm men.

Among these women are prostitutes and poisoners (Sparrow 1970; Pollak 1950; Davis 1937). Providing images of the lustful roots of adult female offending, the early literature also featured sexual promiscuity as the hallmark of delinquency in girls (Vedder and Somerville 1970; Cowie, Cowie, and Slater 1968; Morris 1964; Cohen 1955; Glueck and Glueck 1934; Bingham 1923; Thomas 1923).

Female offenders have been depicted as cruel and revengeful, as a "witch" or a "bitch" (Adam 1914; Lombroso and Ferrero 1895). Violent women may possess some combination of attributes, as in Gerald Sparrow's description (1970) of a female murderer who "made her bow on the stage of history, arrogant, cunning, seductive, cruel, feminine, a daughter of evil, masquerading as a woman of piety" (35).

In other accounts, female criminals are represented as gender-deviant: ugly, anti-family, masculine, lesbian, or anti-male (Chesney-Lind 1999; Dolan 1992). Take, for example, Lombroso and Ferrero's description of a female offender with "gigantic incisors, and down so long as to resemble a beard" (1895, 11), or John Cowie, Valerie Cowie, and Eliot Slater's assertion that delinquent girls are commonly "oversized, lumpish, uncouth and graceless, with a raised incidence of physical defects" (1968, 165). More recently, Ann Goetting (1987) reported that most of the homicidal wives she studied were "obese and in other ways unhealthy and unattractive by media standards" (340).

There is also Freda Adler's now-refuted argument (1975) that the modern women's movement generated a more aggressive female offender whose criminal activity is similar to that of men. Luke Owen Pike's warning nearly a century earlier (1876) was similar: "every step made by woman towards her independence is a step toward that precipice at the bottom of which lies a prison" (527). As Meda Chesney-Lind (1999) points out, women's violence is often represented as a potential challenge to women's domination by men.

Noting the special viciousness of women who kill, Sparrow (1970) noted: "[Female murder] is stamped with that characteristic subtlety and horror that has distinguished the rare evil women of all times" (7). Relatedly, the female murderer may be rendered incapable of "feminine" motivation. Anne Campbell (1993, 144) has pointed out that judges and the media often "try to place a masculine and instrumental interpretation" on female aggression.

Representations of murderous females abound in mythology. Whether in multiples like the sirens and harpies, or alone such as Delilah and Medusa, seductive, man-killing women are legendary (Macdonald 1995; Lederer 1968). Researchers have also noted modern film portrayals of evil women, including "femmes fatales" who seductively entrap men, "black widows" who prey upon their family members, and "she-devils" who are especially treacherous (Macdonald 1995; Birch 1994; Holmlund 1994; Creed 1993). These same authors have also pointed out that violent women are sexually marginalized in mainstream films today. The message is that lesbians and masculinized women are killers, often of men (Van Gelder 1992).

Real cases may be characterized as illustrative of the fictional persona. For example, in a 1989 criminal case in Australia, a woman named Tracy Wigginton reportedly lured a drunk man to an isolated spot with a "promise of sex" and then murdered him. She was dubbed by the press as a "lesbian vampire killer" who had satanic powers (Verhoeven 1994, 97). Played up in the trial and by the media was the sexual relationship between Wigginton and three women who were "under Wigginton's spell" and aided her in the murder.

By virtue of their selection for the death penalty, the women in this study also epitomize female evil. Examination of the accounts of them revealed representations in line with the above stereotypes.

Women on Death Row: The Study

At the end of 1993 there were thirty-five women on death row in the United States, all convicted of capital murder. They accounted at the time for slightly over 1 percent of the approximately twenty-eight hundred persons on death row, and less than 1 percent of the approximately fifty thousand women in prison (Streib 1993). It can be argued that this small, select population represents "worst case" female evil, that is, crimes so heinous as to deserve the ultimate punishment.

Representations of these women were found in newspaper articles, crime and detective magazines, and legal documents. The media accounts typically reflected the prosecutorial point of view and often quoted or paraphrased a prosecutor's comments. Discrepancies within and between media and prosecutorial accounts were limited for the most part to small factual details, such as dates, the spelling of names, and the precise order of events in the crime. The legal documents included appellate briefs and other public-record case material.

In almost half (N=sixteen) of the thirty-five cases, the victim(s) was (were) an intimate other, most commonly a husband or lover (N= eleven). Three women were given the death sentence for the murder of an acquaintance or a significant other. Seventeen of the women had more than one victim, and the majority (N=twenty) did not act alone. Twelve committed the crime in the company of a partner with whom they had affective ties, and eight hired someone else to commit the murder. Fifteen of the death-sentenced women are of color: eleven African American and four Latina. Murders involving an intimate other were overwhelmingly intra-racial.

Representations of women on death row fit with cultural stereotypes described earlier. In accounts supportive of the state's case, attributes of the women were differentially emphasized, allowing for an identification of different types of evil women, represented as: Black Widows; Cold Calculators; Depraved Partners; Explosive Avengers; and Robber-Predators (Farr and Farr 1998).

Black Widows

Three women on death row were referred to as "black widows" in various media accounts. All of these women were white, and all but one of the victims, typically described as innocent and unsuspecting, were white men. These Black Widows all acted alone, and each has persistently denied her guilt.

Reported in more than one article were friends' descriptions of one of the Black Widows as good-looking, a former topless dancer and a current barmaid who used off-color, or "salty" language and had a wicked temper (Cox 1986; Heise 1986). One journalist (Heise 1986) wrote about her: "And thus began a complex web of probing lies by a black widow who actually had her husband build his own grave, then plant flowers on it" (7).

Another of the Black Widows was referred to as a "femme fatale" (Roen 1986) and a "cunning brunette" (Koenig 1985) by the media. Developing the analogy, one journalist (Roen 1991) reported that "the Black Widow spun a lethal web around her loved ones and effectively neutralized them with deadly poison" (39). One witness testified that he had sex with her the night of her victim-husband's funeral, and another testified that she had seen the defendant fake emotions on many occasions (Koenig 1985).

During her trial, a third Black Widow was described as good-looking, a flirt, cold, manipulative, and as "wearing too much make-up" (Oriole 1990). Witnesses testified that she had shown no emotion over her victim's death (Griggs 1992).

Cold Calculators

Ten women were convicted of a decidedly unfeminine act: murdering a significant other solely for financial gain. Similar to the first category, these women were portrayed as cold and heartless, cunning and manipulative. Unlike the Black Widows, however, the Calculators were not serial killers who appeared to choose their victim unpredictably and without clear motivation. Rather, the motivation of the Calculators was said to be financial gain.

Eight Calculators were white, as were their victims in seven cases. The victim was typically a husband or lover, and in seven of the ten cases, the woman had hired another man to kill her loved one. Victims were frequently depicted as innocent and undeserving of their fate. One victim-husband, for example, was described as "quiet and introspective," and as happiest when he was "puttering around the house" or feeding the horses on their small farm (Radner 1989).

In one case, a neighbor testified that the defendant was no "goody two shoes," saying that he often saw her sneak off for an all-night rendezvous while her husband worked the night shift (Sharpe 1989). One of the co-defendants testified that he, the defendant, and the defendant's boyfriend sat around and drank beer after her husband had been murdered, and that she had then given him one of her husband's jogging suits (Sharpe 1989).

Another Calculator was described as an adulteress who murdered her husband with her boyfriend's gun (Elliott 1988). In yet another case, the woman's boyfriend was with her when she murdered her husband; both perpetrators were described as drunk and on drugs at the time of the crime (Sjostrom 1992). In a fourth case, a Calculator was convicted of beating to death her elderly husband, who was reported to be senile and helpless (*Charlotte Observer* 1993). Included in the trial was graphic testimony about injuries to the victim's genitals (*Charlotte Observer* 1990).

Genital mutilation was also a factor in another Calculator's case. Here, a co-defendant testified that the woman hired him to murder her male roommate and told him to mutilate the victim's genitals so that the murder would appear to have been the result of a gay men's quarrel (Lasseter 1991). The perpetrator and the victim were said to be regulars at neighborhood gay bars.

Depraved Partners

Also negatively stereotyped was the explicitly sexual, but risk-taking and ruthless younger woman—an embodiment of evil—linked sexually and criminally with an evil male partner. Depraved women and their male partners typically engaged in a serial spree of thrill-murders, most commonly of young women. Five of the condemned women, among the youngest of the thirty-five women, exemplify this type. Four of the five are white. ·

The male crime partner of one of these women was affiliated with white supremacist groups, his alignment expressed through a swastika tattoo on his "muscular" body (Kelly 1989). The woman in this case was described by the prosecutor as manipulative, clever, and reeking of sexuality (Wride 1992), and a *Los Angeles Times* reporter (Wride 1992) commented further on her appearance: "Slim and pretty with brown hair spilling down her back, . . . [she] wore lipstick and mascara and appeared in good spirits, smiling and laughing with ease during a two-hour interview" (A3). Her partner called her "Cynful," and she called him "Squeeze."

Describing another Depraved woman's appearance in court, one journalist wrote: "Dressed in a flowered blouse, her hair curling about her shoulders and smiling, she was accompanied to court" (Murray 1983). This couple also exchanged nicknames: he referred to her as "Lady Sundown," and she called him "Night Rider" (Koenig 1984).

In another Depraved case, the perpetrator testified at her trial that her boyfriend often talked of killing people, "like assassin work," and said that he would turn her into the "best hit-woman around" (Rust 1992; Nina Cox 1985b). Their "wedding" snapshot showed them sitting atop a Harley-Davidson motorcycle, with the "groom" wielding a shotgun (Lowry 1992). Identified by one journalist as "Houston's Horny Pick-Axe Murderess" (Walker 1984a), she was further described as an "attractive brunette" (Nina Cox 1985b), and as having "charcoal-colored eyes and thick tumble of hair [that] give her a faint gypsy appearance" (Rust 1992). This woman was executed in Texas in 1998, the first woman to be executed in the United States in almost fifteen years.

In the fifth case, a woman and her male companion conceived a plan to torture and murder two male acquaintances. In between the murders, according to the prosecutor, she sat down to eat doughnuts (Bill Cox 1985a; Taverner 1984; Walker 1984b). She had worked as a topless or nude dancer (Bill Cox 1985a; Walker 1984b), described as part of her pattern of "life on the wild side" (Bill Cox 1985a).

Two other women were convicted along with their male partners of multiple murders, but neither was depicted as sexual or depraved. Rather, their involvement, while presented as intentional and knowing, appeared to be an accommodation to their "evil" male partner.

Explosive Avengers

Ten of the women were characterized as dangerous because of their confrontational, often unpredictable, violence. Depicted both as man-haters and man-like, nine of them were convicted of a single-situation murder; the tenth was convicted of serial murders. Seven are women of color—five African American and two Latina. Of the six cases in which homosexuality was alleged, four are in this category. Although their capital crimes are varied, in each case they are perceived as having been angry or vengeful in committing these murders. In six cases, the offender acted alone. In the four remaining cases, the woman played a lead role in the murder.

In one Avenger case, a black woman shot her lesbian lover in front of a police station, where the lover had fled following a domestic dispute. In another, a Cuban immigrant and her lesbian lover were convicted of the beating murder of the former's three-year-old son. News items about the case featured the perpetrator as not only a lesbian but a cocaine-addicted mother (*Sun-Sentinel* 1992a, 1992b, 1992c; Yanez 1992).

Three of these women murdered acquaintances who they thought had crossed them, or from whom they were seeking revenge (one drug-related and another gang-related). Describing the arrest of one of these women, one journalist (Walker 1984b) reported that the officers took a "cursing, intoxicated [woman] and her son into custody."

Two Avenger women, both self-identified lesbians and prostitutes, were given the death sentence for killing "johns." One, an African American woman, was reported to have spit at the jury following the rendering of the guilty verdict (Mowatt 1992; Racher 1992). Another was described as a man-hating lesbian "hooker," a representation that was to negate her claims that her victims had abused her (Geehr 1992; Roen 1992).

Most of the murders in this category seem to lack significant premeditation. At the least, most are not the kinds of cases that typically result in the death penalty—at least not for white heterosexual women or men.

Robber-Predators

Murder in the course of a robbery is a typical male capital offense, and has been characterized as a "masculine-type" crime (Campbell 1993; Katz 1988). Each of the four Robber-Predators committed her crime alone, and the murders were "hands on" (strangling or beating). Two of these women were African American and one was Latina. Although all were described as drug addicts, most notable was the relative absence of media characterizations of these defendants. More attention was given to the vulnerability of their victims, in two cases elderly persons, and in another a child.

Conclusion

Images of women on death row reflect gender stereotypes of evil women depicted as Black Widows, Cold Calculators, Explosive Avengers, Depraved Partners, and Robber-Predators. These categorical images featured typifications of evil associated with femaleness, as well as masculinized forms of evil in women.

Almost half of the women were on death row for having killed a significant other, typically a husband or male lover, motivated by financial gain. These women were portrayed as manipulative murderers of innocent and unsuspecting husbands or boyfriends. In another category were the five young, "depraved" women, whose evil, along with that of their male crime partner, was juxtaposed against the innocence of their young, hapless victims. The great majority of women in both of these categories were white, as were their victims.

Close to one third of the condemned women were sentenced to die for a murder that appeared more situational than premeditated. They were depicted as hot-tempered, vengeful, and unpredictably violent. Along with the predatory robbers, these "avengers" were largely women of color, or portrayed as lesbian or masculine.

Of interest in itself is the finding that women on death row are depicted by prosecutors and the media either as possessing evil female traits or as gender-deviant. Especially noteworthy is the finding that the former consist largely of white women who kill white male loved ones, and the latter largely of women of color or sexually marginalized women who typically kill strangers or acquaintances.

Having been given the harshest state punishment, women on death row can be treated as examples of "worst-case" evil. Analyses of media depictions of these women and their cases revealed representations that fit with cultural, race-linked stereotypes about evil that is inherently female, as well as evil that emanates from "gender-deviant" women. Such representations provide the public with nuanced caricatures of female evil, to be literally eliminated through the execution of its carrier. The depictions may also have served as an extra-legal aggravating circumstance in the court's capital punishment decisions, as well as a justification of the death sentence after it has been given. This analysis of female evil is consistent with classic sociological arguments about the function of deviance as a social control mechanism. Representations playing on familiar stereotypes inform the public of potential danger and warn women to suppress their evil proclivities and maintain their heterosexual femininity.

Works Cited

Adam, Hargrave L. 1914. *Woman and Crime*. London: T. Werner Laurie.

Adler, Freda. 1975. *Sisters in Crime: The Rise of the New Female Crim*inal. New York: McGraw-Hill.

Becker, Howard. 1963. *Outsiders*. New York: Free.

Bingham, Anne T. 1923. "Determinants of Sex Delinquency in Adolescent Girls Based on Intensive Study of 500 Cases." *Journal of Criminal Law and Criminology* 13: 494-586.

Birch, Helen. 1994. "If Looks Could Kill: Myra Hindley and the Iconography of Evil." *Moving Targets: Women, Murder, and Representation*. Ed. Helen Birch. Berkeley: U of California P. 32-61.

Campbell, Anne. 1993. *Men, Women, and Aggression*. New York: Basic.

Carlen, Pat, and Anne Worrall. 1985. "Introduction: Gender, Crime, and Justice." *Gender, Crime, and Justice*. Ed. Carlen and Worrall. Philadelphia: Open UP. 1-15.

Charlotte Observer. 1990. "3 Women Now on Death Row, Jury Convicted Wife in N.C. Man's Death." 6 Nov.: 14C.

——. 1993. "Death Sentence Upheld for Husband-Beater." 5 June: 2C.

Chesney-Lind, Meda. 1999. "Media Misogyny: Demonizing 'Violent' Girls and Women." *Making Trouble: Cultural Constructions of Crime, Deviance, and Social Control*. Ed. J. Ferrell and N. Websdale. New York: Aldine de Gruyter. 115-40.

Cohen, Albert K. 1955. *Delinquent Boys*. New York: Free.

Cowie, John, Valerie Cowie, and Eliot Slater. 1968. *Delinquency in Girls*. London: Heinemann.

Cox, Bill. 1985a. "A Gurney Ride to Eternity." *Official Detective* Aug.: 18-22, 57-59.

Cox, Nina. 1985b. "The Nude Couple Was Bludgeoned wth a Pick-Axe." *True Detective* July: 24-25, 61-66.

——. 1986. "Murder Mysteries in Gun Barrel City." *True Detective* Aug.: 40-41, 58-64.

Creed, Barbara. 1993. *The Monstrous-Feminine: Film, Feminism, Psychoanalysis*. London: Routledge.

Daly, Kathleen, and Meda Chesney-Lind. 1988. "Feminism and Criminology." *Justice Quarterly* 5: 101-43.

Davis, Kingsley. 1937. "The Sociology of Prostitution." *American Sociological Review* 2: 744-55.

deRham, Edith. 1969. *How Could She Do That: A Study of the Female Criminal*. New York: Clarkson N. Potter.

Dolan, Frances E. 1992. "Home-Rebels and House-Traitors: Murderous Wives in Early Modern England." *Yale Journal of Law and the Humanities* 4: 1-31.

Durkheim, Emile. 1938 [1915]. *The Rules of Sociological Method.* Trans. Sarah A. Solovay and John H. Mueller. Ed. George E. G. Catlin. New York: Free.

Elliott, Janet. 1988. "Woman Receives Death Penalty for Murdering Her Husband, 2 Children." *Houston Post* 26 Oct.: A8.

Erikson, Kai T. 1966. *Wayward Puritans:A Study in the Sociology of Deviance.* New York: Wiley.

Farr, Kathryn A., and Sheila J. Farr. 1998. "Representations of Female Evil: Cases and Characterizations of Women on Death Row." *Quarterly Journal of Ideology* 21: 3-33.

Farrell, Ronald A., and Victoria Lynn Swigert. 1988. "A Hierarchical Systems Theory of Deviance." *Social Deviance.* Ed. Farrell and Swigert. 3rd ed. Belmont, CA: Wadsworth. 391-407.

Ferrell, Jeff, and Clinton R. Sanders, eds. 1995. *Cultural Criminology.* Boston: Northeastern UP. 391-404.

Garfinkel, Harold. 1956. "Conditions of Successful Degradation Ceremonies." *American Journal of Sociology* 61: 420-24.

Geehr, Barbara. 1992. "Aileen Wuornos: Lethal Lesbian Hooker." *True Detective* Oct.: 601-26.

Glueck, Eleanor T., and Sheldon Glueck. 1934. *Five Hundred Delinquent Women.* New York: Knopf.

Goetting, Ann. 1987. "Homicidal Wives: A Profile." *Journal of Family Issues* 8: 332-41.

Goffman, Erving. 1963. *Stigma: Notes on the Management of Spoiled Identity.* Englewood Cliffs, NJ: Prentice-Hall.

Griggs, John. 1992. "Death Row Granny." *Detective Dragnet* Feb.: 10-12, 47-55.

Heidensohn, Frances M. 1968. "The Deviance of Women: A Critique and an Enquiry." *British Journal of Sociology* 19: 160-73.

Heise, Jack. 1986. "Decayed Corpse in the Wishing Well." *Inside Detective* March: 6-10, 60-69.

Holmlund, Christine. 1994. "A Decade of Deadly Dolls: Hollywood and the Woman Killer." *Moving Targets: Women, Murder, and Representation.* Ed. H. Birch. Berkeley: U of California P. 127-51.

Katz, Jack. 1988. *Seductions of Crime: The Moral and Sensual Attractions of Doing Evil.* New York: Basic.

Kelly, Bill. 1989. "Lethal Lovers Rape-Terror Spree." *Inside Detective* Feb.: 36-37, 57-61.

Klein, Dorie. 1973. "The Etiology of Female Crime: A Review of the Literature." *Issues of Criminology* 8: 3-30.

Koenig, Joseph L. 1984. "The Savage Sex Crimes of Lady Sundown and Night Rider." *Master Detective* July: 34-37, 68-72.

——. 1985. "Cunning Brunette's Money and Murder Scheme." *Inside Detective* July: 6-9, 46.

Lasseter, Don. 1991. "Trail of the Gay Mutilator." *Detective Cases* Jan.: 6-22.

Lederer, Wolfgang. 1968. *The Fear of Women.* New York: Grune & Stratton.

Lemert, Edwin M. 1997. *The Trouble with Evil: Social Control at the Edge of Morality.* Albany: SUNY P.

Leonard, Eileen. 1982. *Women, Crime, and Society: A Critique of Theoretical Criminology.* New York: Longman.

Lombroso, Caesare, and William Ferrero. 1895. *The Female Offender.* London: T. Fisher Unwin.

Lowry, Beverly. 1992. *Crossed Over: A Murder, A Memoir.* New York: Knopf.

Macdonald, Myra. 1995. *Representing Women: Myths of Femininity in Popular Media.* New York: St. Martin's.

Madriz, Esther. 1997. *Nothing Bad Happens to Good Girls: Fear of Crime in Women's Lives.* Berkeley: U of California P.

Morris, Ruth. 1964. "Female Delinquency and Relational Problems." *Social Forces* 43: 82-88.

Mowatt, Raoul V. 1992. "Sentenced to Die for Slayings, Prostitute Spits at Jury." *Philadelphia Enquirer* 9 April: B6.

Murray, Benison. 1983. "Murder Wasn't Enough for the Sex-Hungry Couple." *Official Detective* Nov.: 46-47, 60, 62, 64.

Naffeine, Ngaire. 1987. *Female Crime: The Construction of Women in Criminology.* Boston: Allen & Unwin.

Oriole, Frank. 1990. "Arsenic and the Gospel Lady." *True Detective* Aug. 24-27, 38-39.

Pike, Luke Owen. 1876. *History of Crime in England.* Vol. 2. London: Smith, Elder.

Pollak, Otto. 1950. *The Criminality of Women.* Philadelphia: U of Pennsylvania P.

Racher, Dave. 1992. "It's Life and Death for Hooker Crimes." *Philadelphia Daily News* 9 April: 26.

Radner, Henry. 1989. "Killer Who Divided Himself in Two." *Detective Cases* June: 20-21, 40-43.

Reinarman, Craig. 1993. "The Social Construction of Drug Scares." *Constructions of Deviance: Social Power, Context, and Interaction.* Ed. P. A. Adler and P. Adler. Belmont, CA: Wadsworth. 92-104.

Roen, Sam. 1986. "Rx for Riches." *Official Detective* July: 38-41, 68-73.

——. 1991. "The 'Black Widow' Spun a Web of Murder." *Startling Detective* Jan.: 20-23, 50-56.

——. 1992. "Rampage of the Bull-Dyke Man-Eater." *True Police* Dec.: 50-56.

Rust, Carol. 1992. "Amazing Grace." *Houston Chronicle* 14 June: 135: G10-13.

Sharpe, Franklyn. 1989. "Torched Skeleton in the Ravine." *Inside Detective* Nov.: 26-30, 70-73.

Sheley, Joseph F., and Cindy D. Ashkins. 1981. "Crime, Crime News, and Crime Views." *Public Opinion Quarterly* 45: 492-506.

Simon, Rita J. 1975. *Women and Crime.* Lexington, MA: Heath.

Sjostrom, Joseph. 1992. "Child-killer Gets Death Penalty for 2nd Murder—Her Husband." *Chicago Tribune* 10 Oct.: 5.

Smart, Carol. 1976. *Women, Crime, and Criminology: A Feminist Critique.* London: Routledge & Kegan Paul.

Sparrow, Gerald. 1970. *Women Who Murder.* New York: Abelard-Schuman.

Streib, Victor L. 1993. "Capital Punishment for Female Offenders: Present Female Death Row Inmates and Death Sentences and Executions of Female Offenders, January 1, 1973, to May 1, 1993." Unpublished report, available from Victor L. Streib, Cleveland State University.

Sun-Sentinel (Miami). 1992a. "Mother Goes on Trial in Beating Death of Son." 13 March: 4B.

——. 1992b. "Jury Calls for Death." 27 March: 3B.

——. 1992c. "Mother of `Baby Lollipops' Deserves to Die in the Electric Chair, Jury Says." 27 March: 3B.

Tannenbaum, Frank. 1994 [1938]. "The Dramatization of Evil." *Theories of Deviance.* Ed. S. H. Traub and C. B Little. 4th ed. Itasca, IL: Peacock. Reprinted from Crime and the Community. New York: Columbia UP. 293-97.

Taverner, Mason. 1984. "The Sleeping Bag Shrouded Two Rotting Bodies." *Inside Detective* Aug.: 32-35, 54-55.

Thomas, W. I. 1923. *The Unadjusted Girl.* Boston: Little, Brown.

Van Gelder, Lindsy. 1992. "Attack of the 'Killer Lesbians.'" *Ms.* Jan./Feb.: 80-82.

Vedder, Clyde B., and Dora B. Somerville. 1970. *The Delinquent Girl.* Springfield, IL: Charles C. Thomas.

Verhoeven, Deb. 1994. "Biting the Hand That Breeds." *Moving Targets: Women, Murder and Representation.* Ed. H. Birch. Berkeley: U of California P. 95-126.

Walker, Clarence. 1984a. "Houston's Horny Pick-Axe Murderess." *True Police* Dec.: 24-27, 42-45.

Walker, Wayne T. 1984b. "Mom and Junior Shared the Kill." *Headquarters Detective* Jan.: 10-13, 48-50, 52, 54-55.

Wride, Nancy. 1992. "Condemned and Waiting." *Los Angeles Times* 26 April: A3, A34.

Yanez, Luisa. 1992. "Child's Killer Pleads for Mercy, Baby Lollipops' Mom Could Get Electric Chair When Judge Sentences Her Today." *Los Angeles Times* 1 April: 3B.

4

RECONSTRUCTING THE REALITY:
UNWANTED MEMORY IN THE COURTROOM

Yiwei Chen

Memory is not an instrument for exploring the past but its theatre.
—Walter Benjamin (1892-1940), German critic and philosopher

Memory As a Theater or an Instrument

There are a lot of metaphors of memory: a warehouse that stores our past experience, a camera that takes static snapshots of our environment, or a working desk that only keeps materials relevant to our current task. Walter Benjamin suggests that memory is not an instrument that we use to explore the static past. Instead, memory is a theater of the past, "a dynamic medium of experience imbued with drama and feeling, and invigorated by the inherently human capacity for narrative creation" (Lynn and Payne 1997, 55). As a consequence of this metaphor, we can infer that memory is not a simple recording of what happened in the past. Rather, memory is reconstructive, can be shaped by present interests, goals, and beliefs, and may be inaccurate or even false.

However, sometimes memory is the only instrument available for exploring what really happened in the past. For example, justice in American criminal trials has relied heavily on evidence, or all the testimony received from the witnesses in the courtroom (Ohio Jury Instructions 1994). Twelve members of the jury have to decide the disputed facts beyond reasonable doubt. The definition of *reasonable doubt* is given as follows:

Reasonable doubt is present when, after you have carefully considered and compared all the evidence, you cannot say you are firmly convinced of the truth of the charge. Reasonable doubt is a doubt based on reason and common sense. Reasonable doubt is not mere possible doubt, because everything relating to human affairs or depending on moral evidence is open to some possible or imaginary doubt. Proof beyond a reasonable doubt is proof of such character that an ordinary person would be willing to rely and act upon it in the most important of his own affairs. (Ohio Jury Instructions 1994, 36)

There are several noteworthy points in the above definition. First, the basis of justice in American criminal trials relies on evidence presented in the courtroom. Second, the court is fully aware that a truth beyond any possible doubt is impossible. In other words, the truth is unknown in the courtroom. And third, judgments of what really happened in the past are based on reason and common sense by an ordinary person.

For the first point, there is an important distinction between evidence and evidence stricken. Evidence stricken by the court and instructed to be disregarded is not evidence and must be treated by the jury as though they never heard it (Ohio Jury Instructions 1994). Can the jury really do that? Can they erase their memory after hearing the inadmissible evidence just like hitting the "Delete" key on a computer keyboard? Psychologists have conducted research, including my own, examining the unwanted effects of the to-be-forgotten information on judicial judgments (Chen 1998; Chen and Blanchard-Fields 2000; Gilbert, Tafarodi, and Malone 1993; Schul and Burnstein 1985).

The second point states that a truth beyond any possible doubt is impossible. This could be meant in a philosophical sense, that the truth is beyond human capacity, or it could be meant in a psychological sense, because human memory and judgments are susceptible to errors and biases. In this essay, I define *truth* in the courtroom using common sense: the critical event that happened in the past. It then follows logically that if members of the jury could physically travel back in time and observe the critical events with their own eyes, they should have a better chance to decide the disputed fact. Unfortunately, the current judicial process at best represents a mental travel to the past: reconstructing the reality based on evidence. Jurors "are the sole judges of the facts, the credibility of the witnesses and the weight of the evidence" (Ohio Jury Instructions 1994, 41). Excluding intentional lies by eyewitnesses, I want to emphasize the memory accuracy of eyewitnesses. How well do eyewitnesses use memory as an instrument to explore the past? Some psychologists (Ceci and Bruck 1993; Loftus, Miller, and Burns 1978) have used an eyewitness testimony paradigm to study the suggestibility of eyewitnesses and the accuracy of their reports. Recent literature on false memories (Schacter 1997) and on repressed memories (Loftus 1993) has shed more light on using memory as an instrument in the courtroom.

Finally, formal American justice processes such as criminal trials require the participation of average citizens who have no formal legal training. In order for the legal procedure to make sense to ordinary persons, criminal trials are usually organized around an implicit framework of social judgments that people bring into the courtroom from everyday life: storytelling (Bennett and Feldman 1981). This format may some-times pose problems to the purpose of American justice system. One major flaw with this process is whether care about the truth or how well the story is told. These two aspects can be closely related but are not always. However, this question does not fall within the scope of this essay.

Discrepancies between the Constructed Reality and the Truth

Memory and judgments based on reconstructed reality in the court-room are, in many important respects, unverifiable in terms of the truth, or what really happened in the past. In order to objectively study the accuracy of the reconstructed reality, we somehow have to know the truth. Psychologists have presented the truth to participants in laborato-ries and then again at later times to compare their memory reports to the known truth.

Biased Eyewitness Testimony

E. F. Loftus and her colleagues (1978) have created a paradigm to study eyewitness testimony in psychological laboratories. The general procedure consists of first presenting participants a critical event to observe, such as a maintenance man with a hammer, and later presenting them with either misleading information, such as that the man had a wrench, or neutral information, such as that the man had a tool. Finally, participants are tested for their memory of the critical event. Results showed that the accuracy of participants' memory reports, or eyewitness testimony, is clearly impaired by exposure to misleading information after the critical events. In fact, participants reported seeing the critical event or details that were presented in the misleading information as if the event and details had occurred in the original episode. D. S. Lindsay (1990) further showed that participants continued to report misinforma-tion from a post-event narrative even after they were told that all such information was false.

Suggestibility of Eyewitnesses

Recently, psychologists have become interested in whether eyewit-nesses actually believe that they saw details that were only suggested by lawyers. The new *remember/know* technique (Gardiner and Java 1993) is used to probe the nature of eyewitnesses' reconstructive memory experience. With this procedure, participants are instructed to indicate that they "remember" having seen the items from the critical event only when they possess conscious recollection of specific details of the items. In contrast, they are instructed to say "know" when the items seem familiar but they do not recollect any specific details about them. M. S. Zaragoza and K. J. Mitchell (1996) found that participants often claimed to "remember" the items from the original event when the items were actually suggested by post-event information, which is just like a lawyer's examination or cross-examination.

Recent evidence indicates that older adults and young children are sometimes more suggestible than adults (Ceci and Bruck 1993; Schacter 1997). This issue becomes especially notable since a number of legal cases starting from the beginning of the 1980s have been tried on the basis of children's uncorroborated testimony involving sexual abuse. M. Bruck and S. J. Ceci (1997) have proposed that interviewer bias is the central driving force in the creation of suggestive interviews. One hallmark of interviewer bias is to gather only confirmatory evidence that is consistent with the interviewer's prior beliefs about the truth. For example, a biased interviewer will not ask children open-ended questions such as "What happened?" but instead will resort to a series of specific leading questions such as "Did he touch your genitals?" Studies showed that children made more errors in response to specific questions (45 percent accuracy) than to open-ended questions (91 percent accuracy). In addition, Bruck and Ceci demonstrated that techniques designed for interviewing children about sexual abuse may be especially suggestive. For example, anatomically detailed dolls are commonly used by professionals when interviewing children about suspected sexual abuse in order to avoid language, memory, and motivational, or embarrassment problems. In one experiment, three- and four-year-old children took a medical examination. Half of them also received a routine genital examination. After the examination, children were interviewed about it and were given an anatomical doll and told to use the doll to show how the doctor touched their genitals. Around 50 percent of the children who had not received a genital examination falsely showed touching on the doll. Furthermore, a number of the children who had received a genital examination incorrectly showed that the doctor had inserted a finger into their genitals even though the pediatrician had never done this.

Susceptibility to Inadmissible Evidence

Even if inadmissible evidence can be stricken by the court, the question is whether during their deliberation the jurors can treat it as though they had never heard it. D. T. Gilbert and his colleagues (1993) have directly studied the influence of inadmissible or false information on judicial judgments. For example, they presented participants a crime report with true and false information printed in different colors: true statements in black and false statements in red. Participants were told beforehand that the information printed in red was fiction or false. Half of the participants searched for a digit "5" appearing on the computer screen, as they read false statements (either exacerbating or extenuating the severity of the crimes), or the interrupted condition. The other half read the statements without performing the digit-search task, or the uninterrupted condition. Then all participants were asked to recommend a prison term for the target criminal, among other ratings. The researchers found that the prison terms recommended by the interrupted participants were reliably influenced by the nature of the false statements but not those recommended by the uninterrupted participants. Further analyses revealed that interrupted participants were more likely than uninterrupted participants to misremember false statements as true. Gilbert and his colleagues argued that because jurors in the courtroom usually attend to a lot of information simultaneously, the interrupted condition was closer to a real-world situation.

This research by Gilbert and his colleagues, however, did not address whether young adults who paid full attention during the task would also be influenced by the false information. In some of my own research (Chen 1998; Chen and Blanchard-Fields 2000), a control group who read only true information was included. We found that young adults under full attention were also influenced by the false information, although in a different direction. That is, they recommended more years in prison when reading extenuating false information and fewer years in prison when reading exacerbating false information. This result may appear to be counter-intuitive. We suggested that adults may have been aware of the influence of false information and tried to correct for it; however, they may have over-corrected it because of the lack of knowledge of the exact magnitude of the influence.

These studies support the argument that even if the court can successfully rule out the inadmissible evidence, jurors may still have a difficult time in disregarding the influence on their judgments of their unwanted memory about the information. Y. Schul and E. Burnstein (1985) have demonstrated that jurors' discounting fails especially when the to-be-ignored arguments are presented in an integrative rather than a discrete manner. These results are consistent with common sense about effective storytelling (Bennett and Feldman 1981).

Two Forms of Memory Representation

The important nature of this memory confusion in the courtroom is that it is "unwanted." That is, the memory errors and biases occur despite the conscious intention of the eyewitness or the juror. The eyewitnesses may have truly believed that they saw the critical events that had never happened. This phenomenon became evident in the study described above (Zaragoza and Mitchell 1996) through the *remember/know* technique. Participants actually claimed that they "remembered" vividly the special details from the original event which were never there.

At the same time, the jurors may have sincerely believed that they successfully erased the influence of inadmissible evidence. For example, my 1998 study combined a traditional source-memory task and the *remember/know* technique to study the reason behind susceptibility to false information. The new technique, *source remember/know,* asked participants to classify statements into four categories: true, false, familiar, or new. Specifically, participants were instructed to say "true" or "false" only if they could consciously recollect the exact color in which the statement was printed in previous reports. They were told to say "familiar" if they knew the statement was presented before but couldn't consciously recollect its color. Finally, if they had never seen the statement before, they said "new." I found that both conscious false recollection and a feeling of familiarity accounted for adults' susceptibility to the influence of false information. That is, individuals were more likely to make biased judgments if they either falsely remembered the false information as true or based their judgments on the feeling of familiarity of the false information.

L. L. Jacoby (1991) has proposed that there are two parallel memory processes: conscious and unconscious. Conscious memory process, or recollection, reflects the operation of an episodic memory system that enables retrieval of specific information about a prior encounter with an item, such as remembering the specific details or the exact source of the item. Automatic, or unconscious, memory process, on the other hand, gives rise to an undifferentiated feeling of familiarity. These two memory processes sometimes act in concert to facilitate our memory of past experience and sometimes oppose each other when selective response based on our intention is needed.

For example, when we use memory as an instrument in exploring our past experience in the courtroom, both conscious and unconscious memory processes can act together. The feeling of familiarity of the past occurrence of a critical event could well be correct and thus facilitate our memory or judgments of a particular case. However, sometimes we are asked to provide specific details of a critical event, such as eyewitness testimony, or to differentiate inadmissible from admissible evidence, which it is up to the jury to do. These kinds of tasks demand conscious recollection to oppose the confounding effects of the feeling of familiarity. When conscious memory process fails to oppose the unwanted unconscious memory process, memory errors and biases occur. In everyday life, these memory errors and biases could be taken lightly, or even become a harmless joke. But in the courtroom, consequences of these memory errors and biases could mean life or death for the accused.

In conclusion, it is important to recognize that memory is a reconstructive theater of our past experience, shaped by present interests, goals, and beliefs. There are two qualitatively different memory processes: conscious and unconscious memory processes. When we use memory as an instrument to explore the past, sometimes these two memory processes act together to form our judgments, which at times produce errors.

Works Cited

Bennett, W. L., and M. S. Feldman. 1981. *Reconstructing Reality in the Courtroom*. New Jersey: Rutgers UP.

Bruck, M., and S. J. Ceci. 1997. "The Suggestibility of Young Children." *Current Directions in Psychological Science* 6: 75-79.

Ceci, S. J., and M. Bruck. 1993. "The Suggestibility of the Child Witness: A Historical Review and Synthesis." *Psychological Bulletin* 113: 403-39.

Chen, Y. 1998. "Unwanted Memory: Age Differences in Susceptibility to the Influence of False Information on Social Judgments." Ph.D. diss., Georgia Institute of Technology, Atlanta.

Chen, Y., and F. Blanchard-Fields. 2000. "Unwanted Thought: Age Differences in the Correction of Social Judgments." *Psychology of Aging* 15: 475-82.

Gardiner, J. M., and R. I. Java. 1993. "Recognizing and Remembering." *Theories of Memory*. Ed. A. Collins, M. A. Conway, S. E. Gathercole, and P. E. Morrie. Hillsdale, NJ: Erlbaum.

Gilbert, D. T., R. W. Tafarodi, and P. S. Malone. 1993. "You Can't Not Believe Everything You Read." *Journal of Personality and Social Psychology* 65: 221-33.

Jacoby, L. L. 1991. "A Process Dissociation Framework: Separating Automatic from Intentional Uses of Memory." *Journal of Memory and Language* 30: 513-41.

Lindsay, D. S. 1990. "Misleading Suggestions Can Impair Eyewitnesses' Ability to Recall Event Details." *Journal of Experimental Psychology: Learning, Memory, and Cognition* 16: 1077-83.

Loftus, E. F. 1993. "The Reality of Repressed Memories." *American Psychologist* 48: 518-37.

Loftus, E. F., D. G. Miller, and H. J. Burns. 1978. "Semantic Integration of Verbal Information into a Visual Memory." *Journal of Experimental Psychology: Human Learning and Memory* 4: 19-31.

Lynn, S. J., and D. G. Payne. 1997. "Memory As the Theater of the Past: The Psychology of False Memories." *Current Directions in Psychological Science* 6: 55.

Ohio Jury Instructions. 1994. *Ohio Jury Instructions: Volume Four Criminal.* Cincinnati: Anderson.

Schacter, D. L. 1997. "False Recognition and the Brain." *Current Directions in Psychological Science* 6: 65-70.

Schul, Y., and E. Burnstein. 1985. "When Discounting Fails: Conditions under Which Individuals Use Discredited Information in Making a Judgment." *Journal of Personality and Social Psychology* 49: 894-903.

Zaragoza, M. S., and K. J. Mitchell. 1996. "Repeated Exposure to Suggestion and the Creation of False Memories." *Psychological Science* 7: 294-300.

5

VIRTUAL IMAGINATIONS REQUIRE REAL BODIES

Dena Elisabeth Eber

[D]reams are manifestations in image form of the energies of the body in conflict with each other. . . . The brain is only one of the organs.

—Joseph Campbell

Mind, Body, and VR

According to Campbell, dreams are the foundations for myth, and both impart a level of consciousness that informs the living world. That consciousness, Campbell explains (1988), exists in the body as well as the mind, and it is only a misconception propagated by the Cartesian point of view that knowing is exclusive to the brain. Thus knowledge and existence are dependent upon our body, and no matter where we go, be it in our dreams, a meditation, imagination, or unexplored frontiers defined by new technologies, our bodies are with us.

Among the new frontiers defined by digital technologies are virtual reality (VR) works of art, also referred to as virtual spaces or virtual environments (VE).[1] Many new media artists are exploring digital technology and the body through means other than VR, such as interactive video installations, robotics, World Wide Web art installations, and digital animation. *Body Mécanique* was a recent exhibition at the Wexner Center for the Arts in Columbus, Ohio, devoted entirely to this notion (see Rogers 1998). By VR works of art I specifically mean expressive installations that are real-time stereoscopic (true three-dimensional display): projections which are immersive, interactive, and adapt to a user's movements in space (Durlach and Mavor 1995). Within this synthesized digital space, the user interacts with and experiences three-dimensional (3D) spatialized sound and stereoscopic images which are responsive, in many cases, to her or his head and hand movements. Thus, the imagery and sound change as the user alters both head orientation and physical position in the digital environment. The VE may instead, or also, track hand or other body movements, depending upon the peripherals. These works of art are produced using VR technology such as off-the-shelf head-mounted displays (HMDs) or unique devices that provide a sense of immersion or collect some kind of user input. (For a detailed discussion about VR technology, see Kalawsky 1993.)

The term VR is often overused and tends to conjure up grandiose notions that far surpass its capabilities. It is sometimes associated with ideas such as virtual sex, virtual communities, and to some, disembodiment. Those that uphold the notion of disembodiment claim that works of art which embrace VR technology necessarily encourage a state that affirms the Cartesian duality. Propagated in Western culture during the scientific revolution of the seventeenth century, this duality maintains that the mind is separate from and master over the body and that knowledge is situated in the brain, thus leaving the physical realities of the earth, nature, and flesh behind. This view coincided with attempts to mechanize the organic and to dominate nature, which includes earth, animal and sexual drives, and the body, all identified as female (Merchant 1980). The Cartesian view has oozed into contemporary Western culture, still privileging the mind over the body, especially in VR, a space where users can apparently leave their bodies behind and exist in a purely intellectual and rational realm. This split positions the ground for a belief that artworks made with VR tools disembody viewers and propel them into a pure cyber state.

Although this "Gibsonesque"[2] scenario is rich with metaphors and metaphysical implications, I suggest that any virtual space is an embodied experience because the imagination of the artist and the viewer refer back to the body, to nature, and to the earth. The mind cannot be separated from the body; rather, the two are inextricably intertwined. From the corporeality of the earth and our bodies, we may understand and perceive many more realities, perhaps facilitated by virtual space art installations. In fact, I maintain that even the virtual is real: it is a perception that is a real experience. That perception makes reference to our encounters with the physical and to our flesh.

On Becoming Enlightened

The Enlightened philosophical movement of the seventeenth century, which is characterized by the importance of human logic and reason over the illogical quality of nature, was in part a product of René Descartes's notion of existence: "I think, therefore I am." The Enlightenment theory further assumes that knowledge resides in the rational brain and, because it is objective and independent, it is separate from our world and our bodies and is essentially disembodied (Seidler 1998). Our bodies are thus part of nature, which, according to Enlightenment theory, is something to mechanize and have power over.

Up until the 1600s, Western society valued the parts of the human body and understood that they worked together, the brain included. This was part of an organic philosophy that respected nature as a living organism. Nature was gendered female, it was nurturing and motherly, satisfying the needs of human kind (Merchant 1980). However, nature could at times be wild, unpredictable, and the perpetrator of chaos. According to Carolyn Merchant, it was the role of the scientific revolution to perform two functions on nature, to mechanize it and to control or have power over it. Although this belief had its seeds in early Christianity and Platonic philosophy, it is at this time that Western ideas made a profound shift away from organic theory and toward Enlightenment, thus marginalizing nature, the earth, and the body.

The notion of Enlightenment went on to serve as a basis for many philosophical mutilations of nature, which came to include behaviors and events that were disorderly, irrational, illogical, and emotional. Anything emerging from the body, such as feelings and emotion, were external and thus in opposition to the internal rational mind and consciousness. Experience became something embedded in language and the brain, detached from the corporeal. (For a detailed discussion of this transition, see Seidler 1998.)

With the privileging of mind over matter driving Western culture, it is no wonder that the quest for disembodiment, especially that of knowledge, existence, and experience, has manifested itself in the digital realm. There is a desire to use new technology to enter a pure state of consciousness, one that leaves the body behind. *Mind Children* (1988), by Hans Moravec, head of the Carnegie-Mellon Mobile Robot Laboratory, is an example of this desire; Moravec fantasizes about a future when life as silicon replaces that of the organic. He envisions a time when a robot will surgically remove, then implant the information from a human brain onto a computer, thus disposing of the body and imparting immortality to consciousness. Even though it is far from clear how this vision will be manifested using technology, the desire to privilege the mind over the body using technology is apparent. This Enlightened point of view is the driving force behind the notion that VR works of art facilitate a disembodied experience.

Certainly, VR technology provides a new experience for the user, but is that experience completely unconnected with the body? An HMD provides visual and auditory stimulations that are not quite in sync with how the user has experienced his or her world in the past. The user adapts to this new set of cues in accordance with the rest of his or her body. Simon Penny (1994) presents a number of studies that show how humans and animals adapt to new visual and sensorimotor cues. The ones that are most prevalent are those in which the participant makes a temporary adjustment in cognition, much like a user in a VE would experience. He points out that the key to understanding cognition in VR is whether this kind of adaptation is perceptual or proprioceptive. Proprioception gives us the sense that we are in our bodies, where the boundaries of our bodies reside, and how we situate our body in space. We sense this via receptors in our muscles, joints, skin, and other body parts. One essential difference between perception and proprioception is that the former refers to how we make sense of our world and ourselves given incoming data via our five basic senses, while the latter is based on internally stored information distributed throughout our body; memory in our tissues. Adaptation requires both; our senses attempt to understand incoming data by referring back to schema stored throughout our body, schema created through physically lived experiences. Surely, VR produces many kinds of new sensations, but how we make sense of them depends on what we have stored in our bodies and mind. Even if we imagine or sense that our body is missing, it still exists, for without it, we would not be alive to imagine.

Jean Piaget's cognitive development theory (1971) addresses how the thinking process grows through action with the environment, which refers back to stored knowledge. He argues that *activity* with the environment forces people to make changes in their thinking processes. Because a viewer of a VE work of art experiences different motor and perceptual constraints from anything they have thus far learned, the viewer experiences what Piaget called *assimilation* and *accommodation,* both part of *activity. Assimilation* is when we fit new information into what we already know, and *accommodation* is when we alter schemes to make sense of new experiences that don't fit with what we have stored. Both functions require us to act physically with the environment as well as to refer back to physically lived experiences. VE technology is not presently capable of creating an exact replica of our physical world; it presents instead a new experience, a simulation of nothing. Applying the theory of *assimilation* and *accommodation* to comprehending this new experience, it is clear that our understanding depends on the stored accumulation of knowledge that we have developed through lived experiences. Negotiation of the new space presented by VR works of art is thus a team effort of the body parts, its tissues and organs within, including the brain. The mind simply directs consciousness toward an end, but it works in concert with the consciousness of the body (Campbell 1988).

Experience, Feelings, Emotion, and the Body
Embedded in our Enlightened culture is the notion that experience and emotion are not sources of knowledge; rather, they live in language.

This structuralist belief has its roots in the Cartesian notion that knowing, anything we are, our perceptions and our existence, are solely rational and part of the mind, void of the body. Contrary to this creed is Piaget's *assimilation* and *accommodation* theory, as well as John Dewey's idea that we learn, and thus accumulate knowledge, through experience. The learning is continuous as we work and *feel* through a living world. "Experience occurs continuously," he said, "because the interaction of live creature and environing conditions is involved in the very process of living" (Dewey 1934, 35). When we enter a VR work of art, we encounter an abundance of emotions and feelings through our experience, one that is a continuation of our lives up until that moment.

John Dewey believed that experience is not something that is situated exclusively in the rational mind; rather, it is the set of intelligent actions that we make in our world, actions which include emotions and meaning that in turn feed our knowledge, which ultimately exists in our entire self, going far beyond language. The world in a VR installation is another space to understand, and in so doing, we engage ourselves in intelligent actions that elicit thoughts, feelings, and emotion, which are all part of knowledge.

From the perspective of the Cartesian duality, emotion is situated in the domain of the body. However, emotions and feelings are part of knowing because consciousness resides over the entire body. Clearly, knowledge and existence include irrational and illogical thought working together with logic and rational thought. A user immersed in a VR art installation negotiates new experiences that weave thoughts from the mind and body together with emotion and physical sensations. Although most VR works do not tie force-feedback to the interaction of the visual objects, the user still feels the bodily sensations of being on earth: gravity, friction, temperature, the weight of the HMD, and the strain on his or her feet, to name a few. As pointed out by Dewey, Piaget, and Campbell, such sensations, along with emotion and feeling, all work together with the mind and the new visual experiences in order to produce thought and knowledge.

VR works of art are capable of eliciting emotion in the viewer: sometimes joy, often intense fear or sadness. Rita Addison's *Detour: Brain Deconstruction Ahead* (Addison 1997) takes viewers on an emotional journey through a car wreck and the resulting brain anomalies. Larry Hodges's *Phobia* project (Hodges et al. 1995) walks acrophobic patients through VR exposure therapy, eliciting measurable signs of fear and triumph. Margaret Dolinsky's *Dream Grrrls* immerses viewers in a dream, part of which references the body. This is yet another way for viewers to reflect back on their own bodily experiences. A dream, according to Campbell, is the energies of the body in conflict with one another, and Dolinsky's installation reminds us of those energies.

No matter how we attempt to explain disembodied experiences, our body still tags along; after all, our entire being is embodied. Perhaps the split between mind and body is finally melding in our psyche and we need a new way to describe the harmony of the human self. According to Keith Devlin (1997), logic has so far been unable to describe the complexities of human thought. To be rational is not necessarily to be logical because rational action cannot be captured by a set of formal rules. Human cognition is a complex mesh of feelings, perceptions, outside influences, and our world. That mesh includes the body and its experiences in any setting, and human cognition in VR is an example of these complexities. If VR truly disembodied the user, then by the Enlightened view, the user's response would be logical and controlled and lack elements of the body such as emotion, perspiration, or other measures of carnal functions. The works of VR described below show otherwise.

The Body in VR
Emotion As a Bodily Response

Emotion is the first thing I think of when I recall Rita Addison's *Detour: Brain Deconstruction Ahead.* This VR work of art is a CAVE installation, a non-conventional VE setup which is a physical room with stereo projections on three walls and the floor. The viewer's orientation is tracked via a head tracker and the navigation is controlled with a wand. Although many can stand in the CAVE at once, only one person drives the view and actions. *Detour* was on display during the 1994 Association for Computing Machinery's SIGGRAPH (Special Interest Group, Graphics) convention in Orlando, Florida, and is permanently installed at the Electronic Visualization Lab (EVL) at the University of Illinois in Chicago. This work explores Addison's reality of her mental capacities both before and after a car accident. The presentation leaves viewers with an understanding of such a transition by putting them through the emotional ordeal of the wreck. In this experience, viewers feel passion and a connection with the story. Addison gives viewers a first-hand tour of her photographs before the crash, the crash experience, and the resulting perceptual anomalies after the crash. Through this, she intends that the viewers will feel what some of the brain anomalies were like.

According to viewer testimony, Addison was able to reach this goal, evoking emotion and for some, a special understanding for those that live with people who have similar anomalies. When Addison showed *Detour* at SIGGRAPH 1994, she noted the effect the work had on the viewers, proof that they in fact reached a point of awe with it. One viewer said, "It's a mixture of art, emotion and technology. . . . It literally left me speechless" (Addison 1997, 3). Ben Delaney expressed a mix of emotions when he experienced the work:

Addison's work starts with the accident, then provides a view of the world as experienced through her modified sensorium. Images and sounds are fleeting, moving and often surreal. The experience, though rather beautiful, is frightening, as being trapped in a Picasso painting might be. (Addison 1997, 3)

Delaney's fear was both rational and irrational at once, irrational because the car wreck was not happening to him, but rational because he referred back to his "normal" experiences with cars and "normal" perceptions of the world in order to understand and feel the shift.

When I experienced the installation, I felt the broken glass as tingles throughout my flesh, because my body reminded me of what broken glass feels like through my past lived experiences. For myself, Delaney, Addison, and other viewers of *Detour,* the installation was a lived experience, a continuation of other lived experiences that we understood and knew by using our entire selves.

Anxiety As a Bodily Response

Another virtual environment that elicits carnal responses is Larry Hodges's *Phobia* project (Hodges et al. 1995). Although not a work of art, this VE uses standard VR technology, such as an HMD and an electromagnetic head-tracking device. The head-tracker translates the orientation and location of the user's head in space to the computer, which in turn calculates images that are projected to the HMD and coordinated with the viewer's physical perspective. The results from this study are significant because standard VR tools, which have been criticized for their perpetuation of the split between the brain and the body, were used to create an environment to which users responded on a carnal level. Simon Penny argues that the design of these tools were created from an engineering worldview, which is inherently incompatible with how artists work (for a thorough treatment of this perspective, see Penny 1997). In short, this view states that many new technologies are created from a logic-centered mind, and as I have already pointed out, rational humans are not always logical. Thus, the tools do not mesh with the way humans think, especially some of the nonlinear processes involved in creating art. Further, tools such as the HMD do not seek to include the body in ways that the CAVE or other unique VR tools do. Although I agree that a holistic approach to the design of some new technological tools is sorely lacking, they cannot aid us in detaching our bodies from our minds.

The first part of the *Phobia* project sought to cure acrophobic (fear of heights) users of their condition by using VR exposure therapy. Acrophobia is characterized by signs of anxiety around heights, and in some cases, an avoidance of them. In traditional practice, a therapist gradually exposes the patient to greater heights, for example, bridges or windows in high buildings, either by asking the patient to imagine the situation, or by taking them into it. VR exposure therapy exposes the patient to the various height situations instead of taking them to specific places (Hodges et al. 1995).

Upon being exposed to the VE, the patients showed outward bodily signs of anxiety, much like those they display when looking out of a high window or down from a bridge. Many of the participants experienced shakiness, perspiration, heart palpitations, fear, weakness in their knees, butterflies, and tightness in their chest. The experience the viewers were having was a continuation of their lived physical experiences with gravity and the rest of their world. Their cognition was a result of a complex mesh which included their present physical, visual, and mental sensations and a reference back to the knowledge stored in their bodies about sensations surrounding height. The result was a response from the body and the mind and measured in sweat and shakes.

The Dream and the Body in VR

Margaret Dolinsky's *Dream Grrrls* is an immersive CAVE installation about dreams in which the objects encourage the user to participate in the story rather than view it. As Campbell reminds us, dreams are a result of bodily energies, and this work of art uses that very premise as a base for experience. In *Dream Grrrls,* participants begin and end in a labyrinth, a place from where they may enter a number of different worlds, each representing a different type of dreaming.

In one such world, known as *Vessel World,* Dolinsky uses various vessels to represent the body. Dolinsky (1998) sees connections with the vessel and the vagina, especially as a part of the process of love-making. The vessel is thus an extension of the vagina in bodily form. The vessels reside in a land she refers to as "a desert island of loneliness" and they appear in diverse ways such as ancient, broken, and transparent. Some vessels reflect parts of the viewer while others hide things from them.

Most intriguing is the vessel whose gaze seems to follow the user wherever she or he goes. When the participant confronts this vessel, it begins to shake and appears to engulf the user, suspending navigational control, and expelling her back to the labyrinth, much like waking from a dream.

According to Dolinsky, the person who wears the head-tracking glasses can fully exploit kinesthetics by moving around, bending down, and lying on the floor. Users become active participants in a theater of dreams, consequently having unique experiences that they negotiate in reference to lived experiences from their own past, as well as their dreams. The performance is ultimately complete when participants use their entire self, their present mental and physical sensations, as well as the knowledge stored in their minds and bodies, to interact. Of the body in her work, Dolinsky said, "I like to think that my artwork is completed by the action and reaction of the participants experiencing it. For that they need their mind, body and heart." As with all experience, it includes the entire self, and no matter how we try to ignore the body, the vessel will start shaking to remind us it is there.

Conclusion

As we enter the twenty-first century, humans are beginning to see the need for a broader way to understand the complexities of human cognition and experience. No longer can we depend on the notion that we exist because we think, that our mind is the owner of our experiences, and that all we know is located in the cerebral cortex. As the earth begins to warm, no longer can we claim to dominate nature and pretend that mechanization of the organic is the supreme solution. We are not in charge and no matter what we create, we cannot raise our mental existence above it. We live in bodies that are entwined in a complex relationship with all our organs, tissues, bones, and energies, including our brain. Technology cannot and will not take that away, especially VR.

VR works of art are defining a new frontier, one that gives participants new experiences to reflect on, including the location of their bodies. As viewers carry the experiences of their lives with them into VR installations, they continue them and adapt to new perceptions which refer to life, their body, and their experiences in it.

The knowledge and emotion embedded in our flesh reminds us to tingle, then cry and tremble when we experience the shattered glass and the outcome of the story in Addison's *Detour*. The perspiration, shaking, fear, butterflies, and tension that patients expressed when they experienced VR exposure therapy in the *Phobia* project were signs from the body that it was present. Experience is not embedded in language; it exists as we have it, as we put our whole selves into it, and as we recall it through our distributed systems of memory.

We fly through Dolinsky's *Dream Grrrls* because our body knows and remembers what gravity feels like, and we experience these dreams as if they could be our own, the energies of the organs of the body in negotiation. We know because of our body and with our body. Imagination is an extension of knowing, and our imagination triggered by VR works of art depends on our bodies. The VR frontier will help provide new sensations for our minds, bodies, souls, heart, and our entire being to experience and participate in.

Notes

1. For the sake of being brief, I will refer to the space created by virtual environment technology as VR or VE throughout this essay. The term VR is problematic and is in fact an oxymoron. The debate over what to call it is not within the realm of this essay.

2. This term comes from the notion of cyberspace that William Gibson first wrote about in *Neuromancer.*

Works Cited

Addison, Rita. 1997. *Rita Addison.* Online. Available: http://manray.mit.edu/www/rka/rka.html

Campbell, Joseph. 1988. *The Power of Myth.* New York: Doubleday.

Devlin, Keith. 1997. *Goodbye Descartes: The End of Logic and the Search for a New Cosmology of the Mind.* New York: Wiley.

Dewey, John. 1934. *Art as Experience.* New York: Minton, Balch.

Dewey, John, et al. 1954. *Art and Education.* Merion, PA: Barnes Foundation.

Dolinsky, Margaret. 1998. Personal correspondence.

Durlach, N., and A. S. Mavor, eds. 1995. National Research Council, Committee on Virtual Reality Research and Development. *Virtual Reality: Scientific and Technological Challenges.* Washington, DC: National Academy P.

Hodges, Larry, et al. 1995. "Virtual Environments for Treating the Fear of Heights." *IEEE Computer* 28.7: 27-34.

Kalawsky, R. S. 1993. *The Science of Virtual Reality and Virtual Environments.* Workingham, England: Addison-Wesley.

Merchant, Carolyn. 1980. *The Death of Nature: Women, Ecology, and the Scientific Revolution.* San Francisco: Harper & Row.

Moravec, Hans. 1988. *Mind Children: The Future of Robot and Human Intelligence.* Cambridge: Harvard UP.

Penny, Simon. 1994. "Virtual Reality As the Completion of the Enlightenment Project." *Culture on the Brink.* Ed. Gretchen Bender and Timothy Druckrey. Seattle: Bay. 231-48.

——. 1997. "The Virtualization of Art Practice: Body, Knowledge, and the Engineering Worldview." *Art Journal* 56.3: 30-38.

Piaget, Jean. 1971. *Biology and Knowledge*. Chicago: U of Chicago P.

Rogers, S. 1998. *Body Mécanique*. Columbus, OH: Wexner Center for the Arts.

Seidler, V. J. 1998. "Embodied Knowledge and Virtual Space." *The Virtual Embodied*. Ed. John Wood. London: Routledge. 15-29.

6

JESUS' DAUGHTER:

MEMORIES OF CHILD ABUSE REPRESENTED

THROUGH PERFORMANCE

Burton Beerman and Celesta Haraszti

*   *   *   *   *

Jesus' Daughter Libretto

by Burton Beerman,
with interludes and set 5 by R. Brent Beerman

Set One: Crucifixion

Hush, little baby that can't be free
Hush, baby hush don't cry
Your daddy takes your life
   as your mother watches you die
so hush, little baby
   life was never yours to be
and you don't know why.

Did you hear what she said? what she said that I did?
me, the preacher man, what she said that I did?
I saw it on TV, there are groups to help
people like me who have been wrongfully accused.
help stand up and say no, no, I didn't do this.
Why do you accuse me a preacher man?

Father, father, why have you forsaken me?

Ladies dance, dance with crinoline charms
   flowing from your waists
to attract the hulking males for this is your task
your vision of life with locking arms

you sway your honey hips
no reason to ask why me?
why do I dance and paint my lips
to bring this strength to me?
     to me!
Ladies dance, dance with giggling smiles and pouting, fragile steps
as innocent as a bursting drop of dew
     they shake to foot with the gangling stride of
a newly born calf seeking her mother's milk
The ladies dance, dance
Ladies dance, the dance of death.

Interlude One: Choices and impossible decisions.

The bloody body lies powerless for you. Don't be scared. Go on, she
can't hurt you. Watch her hands open up for you. Press a weak heart
she can't move. She's afraid of you. Touch her—hold her, bring her
close. A touch, a kiss, a soft caress, whisper in her ear and let her
know how to think. The bloody body lies powerless, smile while you
touch, hide your eyes then no one will see, no one will know. Crawl,
find devour. Pray—head bowed in obedience to God—whisper the
commandment and devour her, kill her, take her. Don't wait! Don't
stop! Don't think! Go on, touch her because she is yours.

Set Two: Small Talk

Singer:
Holy, holy
     holy, Daddy is God's messenger
And touches you, touches you with the light
Yet you sit so melancholy,
     My holy child
How many get to be Jesus' daughter?
     This is your birthright,
Yet you sit so melancholy.
     Holy, holy, holy, By all that is holy
Forced to be his wife, at the cost of your life.

Why, why, Why do you blame me
I am God's servant
     Why do you wrongly accuse me
When Jesus is my master.

My child, My little child
I placed you on my lap, my favorite
I rocked you, why do you blame me?

Dancer:
Holy, holy
Brother, Brother good
Brother sister
My people
My suckers
Why, why
How can you hurt me so
When I am God's servant?
Why, why
Who do you cry? I don't understand?
Why do you not want to be Jesus' daughter?

Singer:
The young dame had a sister named Rose
Who was misnamed
    For it is she who is the Rose
As Rose should have been named stone
    For a rose is a Rose, is a Rose is a Rose
baptized as the young dame.

Her father in all his misgodlyness stole her being
So she says: And brother and dad left her for dead.

And this little beaming star,

sat in the mud
Muddled and unaware of her noble birthright
Looking into the wisps of the dew and seeing only the weeds;
Mirror, mirror on the wall; have I the right to live at all?

Like a discarded toy she lay broken
In the arms of evil
    As these sightless voices ran their boats
And gave their sermons
Only in the secret of their hearts stopping to admire
Their ability to turn gold into coal.

But almost unnoticed.

At first just the gasp of a cough.
The first heat of her unbreakable will on her cheek
Then whole movements.

This jewel willed herself from the mud
    Unbeaten by evil
And unbroken by the spiritless father
    (*aside: Well, maybe a bit bent*)
She rises. Her scent evident to everyone
Touched by her magic

For a rose, is a rose, is a rose is always a rose
    Is a wonder, is enchantment.

Dancer:
No, no

Singer:
No, no, I remember
clear as a rainbowed sky after a rain
I remember then it vanishes in a wisp

My body remembers

Singer:
I don't understand why you say these things
that aren't true

Dancer:
No, no, no

Singer:
I don't even know what isn't true.
    At least listen to me.
    Hear my feelings

Dancer:
I know my body remembers.
My body remembers and that is something.

As a boy I dreamed of being the arm of the church. Of being
Schweitzer's partner in Africa. Of helping mankind. I lived for my
children. I lived for them.

Gave them everything. Do you think it was easy becoming a doctor with so many children? No!

Evil. This is evil.

I worked endlessly for Jesus. I brought God to the world. I knelt with the Pope and cried for my dead son. Everyone loves me. Just ask any of them. Everyone adores me. Admires me. I have given them eternal life. Hope. Faith. A future. I have given them my presence and walked among them with Jesus at my side. I have shone as any mortal man should shine. I have done nothing. I have done nothing wrong.

Singer:
Holy. My holy child.
So melancholy, holy.

Dancer:
My body remembers and that IS something.

Interlude Two: Again, choices and impossible decisions.

The bloody body lies powerless for you. Don't be scared. Go, she can't hurt you. Wave a hand over the skin, squeeze a soft spot.

Press a finger into a heart and rip until there's blood, rip a chord until a releasssssse. Scream. There's a scream in the dark, but don't worry because it's yours.

There's a scream in the dark, but your ears are shut. Hide your eyes, smile to the flock, squeeze the soft spot until the life slips. There's a monster in the shadows, watch behind and hold her close. You can't let her go. You are the man whom God ordained, bless thee with light, drink the blood, eat body, don't hear the scream. The tears fall without eyes, master of God, ordain thee to thy life.

Set Three: Silent Rage

The dancer as the young woman can now be resurrected from the death that her tragedy brought to her, eventually removing her mask to reveal the authentic self (or is it?). After dancing with renewed energy brought on by rage she speaks to the audience in an accusatory way, asserting, "I didn't know what you meant. That you meant. I didn't know." She repeats these words, ending with the words that finally reveal that she understands what has happened to her, "To kill me."

Set Four: Illusions

Hush, baby, hush don't cry
Your daddy takes your life
    as your mother watches you die
So hush, little baby,
    life was never yours to be
and you don't know why.

Hush, my little baby
    you never had a chance
daddy stole your crown
    and only your body remembers the dance
my sweet thing,
    hushed little baby
that can't be free enough to love me.

Hush, baby hush don't cry
Your daddy takes your life
    as your mother watches you die
so hush, little baby
    life was never yours to be
and you don't know why.

This truth that is ours
    this religion that the earth is round
that beasts don't feel nor have souls as do we
    that the sun always shines
and a silver lining fills the coat of our misfortunes
that what I see is
    and what I don't see is not necessarily not
that right is clear and hate evil
that evil is good and good is evil no
    that good is good
and evil is evil
    no that good is not bad

and evil is wrong, or is it?
How do you know?
   Do you ever ask?
Are there demons watching us
laughing at our ignorance
Like a giant stadium game
and we the players
   and they the free Romans
unenlightened like rats in a maze
bumping into truths
   a blind man catching lightning bolts

symbols
   the ring
big rocks
   and little stardust on the finger
proclaiming this bond, bond?
   This gaggle tribe
with a history of 50,000 years on the plains
It's a symbol,
   it's just a symbol
a symbol
   but very real.

This moment that I know is real no illusions
no symbols but the unadulterated truth
that split second of reality

Drawn from the clouds
   as the plane descends in to where I was raised
given those values like chuga lugging vodkas
force feeding the rest of life.

Set Five: Crucifixion Revisited

Memory flash—frozen time. The scream doesn't die, bow, and pray,
God is coming, the light is approaching, the monster creeps out of
the shadows.

Turn and look at the mirror, see the blood drip from your mouth,
your hand still wet, put it away. Hide everything, don't say a word.

You are the emperor, you are the ordained one, the divine messenger of God, you are clean. Tell them all, you are clean. There is nothing to fear, but don't look in the mirror, don't hear the scream. The scream. Fight the tears, fight the blood. The scream.

Holy emperor, lost choice of survival. Nowhere to turn, but toward the light and melt with the guilt. Fallen angel, mistaken saint.

Mother born without eyes
The screams shattered your mind
But, you had no ears.
Mothers bless and hold their young, but you turn your back while your daughter bleeds. Save her now mother, kill the devil and give your daughter back her heart.

You're scared he'll break out, but he can't move. Watch him in the cage, he can't raise his eyes to yours—he's the one who is weak— kill him.

You're scared he'll tear your soul, scared he'll rip your chest, scared he'll shred your mind. Numbing fear stops the guilt.

Kill the devil and give your daughter back her heart. Weak, spineless coward, save your daughter's blood! Forget about your own blood for once, give your daughter another life, kill the devil!

*   *   *   *   *

Jesus' Daughter is an operatic stage production and video presentation whose subject matter exposes family secrets and presents them as a young woman's living inheritance and her legacy. This compelling drama plunges headlong into the psychological state of an abused young woman searching for healing. She embarks upon a journey toward the regeneration of her soul as we are captivated by the stalwart courage of this young woman determined to reclaim her life against all odds.

CNN *Science and Technology, FutureWatch,* and *Headline News* filmed the behind-the-scenes making of the opera and aired it for multiple international broadcasts, emphasizing the interactive virtual music and video displayed in the composition. CNN maintains a web page for this broadcast. There is a link on www.mustec.bgsu.edu/~bbeerma/ public_html/ to the CNN web page for the opera.

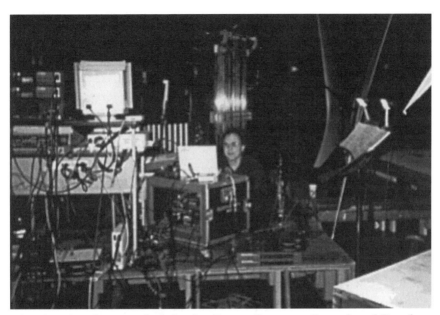

The virtual orchestra and clarinetist, Burton Beerman. From *Jesus' Daughter,* courtesy of the author.

The opera started innocently enough as a brief work for dancer alone called *Silent Rage*. There was no sound. There were only the movements of the solo dancer viewed in silence. Artists have an inner voice that tells them when their work isn't right. It tells them without prejudice, malice, or explanation, and an artist learns to trust this inner voice. He doesn't necessarily share this discomfort with others and certainly he doesn't share it with others viewing his work. *Silent Rage* wasn't right. It worked well enough and was well received by audiences, but the composer and choreographer knew that it wasn't really right, although they wore this concern in silence. This was not a silence between the two of them, though even between collaborators at first there must be a dance. There must be a time of courting in which one collaborator tries to understand the artistic vision of the other in covert communication if not silence.

Silent Rage was first performed in a concert in Palo Alto, California, shared with Chris Jaffe, Director of the Computer Music Center at Stanford, and Fred Malouf, then a Music Synthesis Engineer for Apple. The idea was compelling; at least it appeared silently to sing when first conceived. But then, most creative ideas seem to be glorious when first exposed. The dancer and choreographer, Celesta Haraszti, chose strong, forceful movements, and the work was both impressive and expressive. But the absence of music just did not express whatever was meant by silence. It was a mild cocktail delight composers throw together for the saloon, a past time in which composers often indulge.

The spirit of this silence was not understood but did slowly evolve over several works. The silence was pregnant with an unspoken meaning that would unfold over time and over several different compositions. Its meaning would take shape in the form of a true story about an adult daughter who accuses her father of sexual abuse in childhood. The journey to this final statement was measured and often agonizing. Composers do not necessarily artistically associate themselves with complex social issues but are often the bearers of extravagance, so this was not necessarily a welcome journey.

In the story of the opera *Jesus' Daughter*, who are we to believe? Are we to believe the father, who is a prominent preacher, who considers himself "godlike," above reproach and who denies everything, or do we believe the daughter, who isn't sure what she remembers? Memory deeply buried in her body will not let her rest and feeds her information in terrifying, non-cognitive imagery. As jurors, are we capable of ascertaining the truth? What is the role of the mother, who sits by and doesn't acknowledge anything, although she is not a direct contributor to the abuse? Certainly the body does not invent trauma. Or does it? Or is the body confusing one injury with another? What place was art to have in this complex and true story? What conduits for understanding this tragedy can art provide that the cognitive therapist does not have at his disposal?

A computer-generated music tape was added to *Silent Rage* by composer Burton Beerman, and the combination of the intense percussive computer music and persuasive dance meshed to form an entirely new piece. The title remained *Silent Rage*, even though there was now sound. It was intuitively clear that the word "silent" had a special message, and in time it would reveal itself in other works. This work was performed in this manner several times. It was like the wart on the child that the mother ignores when taking compliments. It was like the unspeakable blemish that one feels but does not express. Artistically it worked and was a dynamic performance vehicle for dancer Celesta Haraszti, yet something was missing, an ominous imminence that was lurking, unspoken but felt, ready to unveil itself, but how?

An artist is not restrained by the empirical guidelines binding the scientist in search of his truth. He is not limited by practical decisions and restricted senses. He is not confused by conventional thought and ideas nor is he misdirected by the inaccurate messages surrounding him. An inner clock, an inner vessel that has its own sense of right and wrong, truth and lies, directs him. He pounds out a picture of reality that can

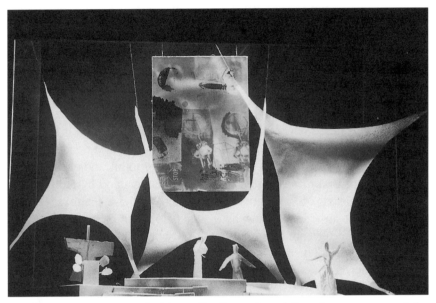

A model of the stage and video sails. From *Jesus' Daughter,* courtesy of the author.

only be seen in parallel universes not directly available to us in this world. When he creates, the hand of God guides him.

Illusions, for electric clarinet, percussion, computer music, and solo dancer, was the next large, theatrical work created by Burton Beerman and Celesta Haraszti. The clarinet was amplified and inserted into a pitch-to-MIDI converter, which allowed a computer to record phrases played by the clarinet and gave a medium by which the clarinet could control the entire computer music environment. In order for the dancer to play several different roles, she carefully changed masks as part of the choreography. This concept found its way into the opera *Jesus' Daughter*, in which both the singer and dancer performed multiple roles, sometimes changing characters by changing masks, and sometimes changing roles simply by assuming a different characterization.

At first, there was no apparent link between *Illusions* and *Silent Rage*. In length, style, and tone they contrasted sharply. One work was a short dance piece with simple technical resources and the other a longer dance exposition with much more complex real-time music and technical media. But the link between these works was the gradually emerging story of the young woman and her father. It wasn't that these works simply assumed the story, but somehow the story was part of both works from their inception. The creative process is more intuitive than quantitative. Ideas come from the artist in ways that at first even he doesn't understand but with maturity learns to trust. The artist's work is a process more than a product, and the magic infused into this final artifact is only possible when the artist trusts his own nature and intuition.

Artistic truth is at once mystical and only understood by the artist who is given this certainty by his inner voices. It is an inner voice, a schizophrenic whisper into his ear by a god deeply buried in his soul, and this is a voice that he learned to trust above all else because it never lies to him. It never betrays his faith nor ever abuses his quest for truth. It is the hand that shapes the form of his work and gives it content, and it is the megaphone that shouts his artistic message to his audience, a message with words, a message that we can only understand by feeling it. It is up to the listener to relinquish any barriers to these feelings, take in what can be absorbed, and use whatever is helpful for the moment.

Silent Rage eventually evolved into a work where the silence was broken both metaphorically and technically, in which the dancer wore a wireless microphone and toward the end of the piece spoke to the audience. At first her words were innocuous, but they were chosen to be provocative. She would challenge unsuspecting members of the audience with such phrases as "YOU! yes, you! ATTACK! USE, ABUSE, IT HAP-PENED TO YOU? WHY ME? WHY ANYONE? NOOOOOOO!" She would visibly rage and strike out at individual audience members, sponta-neously raging at people who were accidentally caught by a spotlight. At certain performances certain chosen members of the audience responded back to the stage, denying any and everything, showing mock anger at the young woman's attacks and accusations. *Illusions* also incorporated the microphone as well as the masks, and both transformed the young woman's personality from the victim to the victor. It gave the dancer a way to show strength and aggressive rejection of the abuse. *Silent Rage* was performed in this manner at the DIA Art Foundation in New York City. In a small and intimate theater the dancer flashed the beams of flashlights into the eyes of the audience in the dark, making her look like a demon emerging from the darkness. She verbally confronted them, demanding that they explain their unspoken actions. She was so close to the audience in such an intimate setting that her confrontation was partic-ularly striking and unexpected. *Silent Rage* was starting to have a charac-ter. It was starting to feel right but it wasn't as of yet wed with *Illusions*.

It was these provocative challenges to the audience by the dancer, demanding to know what they have done and why they did them, that opened the way to the completion of *Jesus' Daughter*, a Techno-Interme-dia Opera in five sets or scenes. This was not an opera in the traditional sense. There was only one singer, and she assumed the identity of sev-eral characters. In addition, she sang in concert with a quartet of virtual singers that were samples of her own voice, and both the dancer and singer spoke in rhythmic patterns reminiscent of rap. Using the model of *Illusions*, the clarinetist was conductor for the ensemble and determined when computer music events occurred. The clarinetist would trigger the quartet of sampled voices with the sound of the clarinet that accompanied the singer and then the soloist would respond in real time. Again, using *Illusions* as a model, the battery of acoustic percussion completed the musical ensemble.

A single dancer wore a wireless microphone as she did in *Silent Rage* and *Illusions*. When both the singer and dancer spoke using a rap-like technique, they were accompanied by virtual choruses speaking in this rhythmic style (not unlike the virtual singing quartets). The singer and dancer both were often the subjects of real-time video projections and the dancer at the crucifixion scene actually controlled the processing of projected video with her dance movements. In addition, her costume is equipped with contact microphones, sensors and receivers that enable her to interact directly with the sound environment. Her body becomes an alternate controller making sound, generating video images, navigating through a virtual space. All of these virtual techniques had to be seamless and appear to be a natural extension of the action on stage. If they ever had a life of their own, then the work would be technically and not artistically driven, and this would not be acceptable.

The stage included three large, sail-like projection screens for both real-time and prepared video. The real-time image of the dancer was most often projected onto these screens in an environment in which her movements most poignantly spoke of untold and unclaimed abuse. The virtual dancer (the counterpart to the live performer) navigates through the virtual environment of her mind and is projected onto four gigantic sails constructed of special super-absorbent fabric that also physically change shape over time into new abstract shapes. This was particularly significant in the opening scene, in which the singer is obviously under attack, but the audience is not clear as to exactly what is happening. It gives the dancer an opportunity as a dancer to link movement and the body of the victim with the abuse. What we know of her plight we know only from her body. The real-time video processing of the dancer allowed the work to show the horrors of the story and still not give it a specific context, for if the dancer herself does not really understand what happened, then how can the audience?

Both the dancer and singer carry out this sense of confusion and paranoia in the opera by using extreme characterizations in their multiple virtual roles. Each is father, mother, and daughter at different times. Included in this mix are two large, fifteen-foot puppets, each one requir-

The father mask worn by the dancer. From *Jesus' Daughter,* courtesy of the author.

The father mask worn by the singer. From *Jesus' Daughter,* courtesy of the author.

ing two people in clear view to manipulate them. One puppet represents the offender, the father/god. He is as inauthentic as you can get. As Pinocchio was (albeit on a *much* lighter note), so is the father/god—inhumane. He is inhumane because he lacks true personhood, he lacks a conscience. The other fifteen-foot puppet represents the beautiful alter-ego of the young woman who views herself as hideous. In one scene, the over-sized woman puppet approaches from behind the singer playing the role of the daughter. As the beautiful puppet stands behind her for all of the playing the audience to see her beauty, she tearfully says, "Mirror, mirror on the way, have I the right to live at all?" There is, it seems absolutely no possible hope for the victim of evil in this play. The perpetrator of evil must supply love, confession, deep remorse, shameful guilt and acknowledgement of violent wrongdoing against one who is in deep need of protection—ones own child. The mother can help somewhat, if she were to respond to her daughter's cries, but unless the father has personhood, the daughter wails at mere animated matter. She needs a person, she needs a person big enough to match her despair.

The full opera is one hour and twenty minutes in length and is in five sections. Gradually, what grew out of the improvised challenges by the dancer to the audience in *Illusions* and *Silent Rage* took shape. Its finished version includes five sets or sections, two of which are *Silent Rage* and *Illusions*. It is not clear, even today, exactly when the story was solidified. The libretto representing the verbal expression riveted through the artist's hands in a hauntingly agonizing manner, yet the words flowed and it was finished in a rather short period of time. The dancer's flesh froze in time and her skin wore the garb of the violated young woman. The process for the dancer was to embody the experience this young woman must have been going through and to traverse the journey of reclaiming her right to be. The composer and choreographer spoke to audience members from performances of *Illusions* and *Silent Rage*. Many people came forth at their own choice and talked about the horrors that they had with abuse. They were children who were afraid to come forth and talk about their tragedy until they saw the individual works or the finished opera. They were people calling in to radio talk shows. It is one of the few aspects of private life that seems to be equally shared by people of all races, classes, family structures, and ethnic backgrounds. They told of their horrors and many described the final opera as a gift, a conduit to their reclamation in ways that therapy did not provide.

The story of the young woman whose body remembered undefined horrors from her childhood, horrors that speak of rape and abuse, emerged. These horrors revealed themselves in ways that she continued not to understand, yet these horrors are living inside her, alive as if they were a mass of parasites attached to her very soul, eating, eating, eating away—never quenched, never scared away, never beaten away from its helpless host. Her memory was not distinct and clear in terms of events, but her body remembered. Her father was a preacher with an international reputation who commanded enormous respect. The father deflects all accusations, but he does it in a way that does not directly deny them. He states, "Why would anyone not want to be Jesus' Daughter?" However, the strong, involuntary feelings brought to the surface in the form of body memory would not let issues rest.

On one level *Jesus' Daughter* is a simple story of incest and abuse, but on another level it is the story of repression and one's journey to reclaiming life from this subjugation. *Jesus' Daughter* is a techno-opera for virtual musical and virtual reality video environments in which the movements of the dancer and performance of the clarinetist control musical and video events. Technology in this work is a tool that functions as a conduit to our souls, that allows us to feel raw emotions that we would otherwise choose to hide. It allows us to experience vicariously these complex emotions in a way that is safe as a work of art and yet powerful and penetrating. *Jesus' Daughter* articulates many diverse technologies in a way that is immediate and direct. Most important, the technology is transparent to the artistic experience, the better to expose the story of the young woman, for if you are infatuated with the technology for its own sake you are not enraged by the tragedy.

The opera uses the religious metaphor of the Crucifixion and Resurrection as a model for this universal story, the Crucifixion being the ultimate violation of a human being and the Resurrection being the final reclamation. In the opening scene we see the young woman in enormous torment, her voice distorted by electronics and her image distorted by real-time video effects. The woman utters primal sounds and the choreography distorts her body in pain. It isn't until the end of the five-minute section that the woman utters words that we can understand. With her body placed on a virtual cross on the video sails, she clearly pleads, "Father, father, why have you forsaken me?" This sets the tone for the first half of the opera.

"Small Talk," the first newly composed and largest section of the opera, provides a space for the daughter to confront the father. At one point, the singer (wearing a "father" mask) warmly cradles his daughter and then he warmly sings to her. In another, the daughter takes the "father" mask (also the face of the puppet father) from the singer, assumes a position behind a pulpit and gives a moving personal declaration of his goodness. Her voice is often painfully distorted and video allows us to see beneath this ruse with grotesque, projected video processing. The dancer ends this sequence by slipping into a robe held on a cross with Velcro. The music becomes angelic, and the dancer holds out her hands as if to bless the audience as Jesus, but then speaks in a devil's processed voice, "I have done nothing. I have done nothing wrong."

One by one young children enter, singing the hymn-like tune of the singer, but with the innocence and purity of children's voices. The daughter collapses and is wrapped and held by the children, ending the section with the declaration, "My body remembers and that IS something." As she weeps the section ends.

The children lovingly carry the woman to a chamber from which the woman cannot escape, and she is electrocuted with special effects caused by special robotic lighting. The woman collapses as the singer reads statistics to the audience about rape over the sad wail of a virtual string instrument.

"Silent Rage" is the set where the young woman is at the cusp of becoming empowered, at the twilight of reclamation and resurrection. It is the section where the young woman reclaims her identity after death, for rape kills a child. It is a living death. It steals her individuality and character and leaves her without any self-worth, sense of self, or hope. Perhaps the only possibility for hope, for life to be authentically regained by the victim, can come from the offender. The offender, the father/god is, however, a puppet. Perhaps death itself would relieve one of this unlucky curse? Evil, and its destructive effects, is the cause of our deepest pains. A young girl moves to the dead woman and gives a rose, infusing her with life and the strength to rise and reclaim her own life. She ends this display of strength and confrontation in "Silent Rage" in a show of lights and effects where she declares, "I didn't know. Didn't know you meant. I didn't know you meant to KILL ME."

"Illusions" follows the strong choreography of "Silent Rage," where the young woman does not wilt from her confrontation as she did in "Small Talk." Her gestures are bold, muscular, and powerful. She then collapses in exhaustion and anger. "Illusions" is a showcase for the dancer to display her newly found strength. She ends the movement by removing her mask, revealing her real face and declaring, "You can not do this to me anymore."

In the last section of the opera the mother is brought to the stage from the audience. The music is sarcastic and carnival-like. The clarinetist leaves his position at the music ensemble behind the sails and serenades the mother up the stairs to the middle of the stage like the pied piper, enticing her to join the father puppet and daughter on stage, against her better judgment. The puppet image of the father was brought to the fair with princely music, and he also is not happy to be trapped in this confrontation. Again, he shows no remorse and his puppet gestures are those of a victim and not an assailant. The daughter demands that the mother choose between the father and her. Not to choose and to be passive is an active choice to kill her. To sit by and watch abuse take place without taking action to stop it is an aggressive act that allows it to continue.

The last set was omitted from the video opera form of the work, which was designed for installation at museums or video showings at festivals. It ended with the clarinetist (who at one point played the role of the father) now playing the role of a male observer, pointing his finger at the camera. It is a close-up, so one can see the fire and anger in his face and hear it in his voice as he declares to the father, "You. You. Yes, you. You are the one." The artist does not judge, but provides a window from which others can decide what is true and what is not true. His work is a gift filled with conduits to unspeakable experiences and understanding not bound by words. It is healing, comforting, perhaps disturbing, yet reassuring, but it never lies.

The impact of the work on victims of abuse of all kinds astonished the creators of *Jesus' Daughter*. It gave credence to the cliché that art is a universal language. It brought young girls violated by their fathers and/or by others known to them at least one step into the light from their shells. Perpetrators wanted to come forward to take part in discussions. This request was most often ignored, as it was viewed as self-serving, voyeuristic, and intimidating.

Psychologists, psychiatrists, psychotherapists, and even philosophers did not immediately embrace *Jesus' Daughter*. They viewed it as territorial invasion, and felt that artists were on dangerous ground that they didn't understand (as if therapists really understood). They ignored the responses that the work elicited from victims; responses that their own probing had trouble penetrating (like a pencil trying to get through concrete). One psychologist at a university stated that they didn't want to participate because they just focused on date rape only. When her objections were further explored, she stated that if they supported this work too many students would come forth and they would then have to take care of them. They found it a better choice to keep the victims suppressed. A safe place manned by qualified professionals was always provided for staged performances of the work, and these therapists were kept very busy.

Artistic expression has a particular meaning for victims of trauma whose experience is encapsulated in the nonverbal sphere, unavailable to language formulation and, therefore, unable to be shared. This extreme sense of isolation is one of the most devastating aspects of trauma. Artistic expression allows the person to give form and substance to the non-verbal experience of horror, pain, betrayal, sorrow, rage, and grief.[1]

The message of *Jesus' Daughter* from "Small Talk" to the end is that life for the victim of incest is an experience of horror, because of the confusion of identities conveyed by the wearing of masks, of being and wishing to be dead, or of being dead while alive. The opera uses masks, puppetry, and computer-controlled musical and video environments to explore the themes of denial, trust, betrayal, and the responsibility of society. When one is the innocent victim of an indelible wrong committed on one's very soul by the very person who is supposed to nurture, only death itself can bring relief. The offender, the father/god-like beast, is presented as a puppet, as a singer and dancer with masks, and as virtual images in projected video, but he is never presented as a flesh-and-blood person. Only the dancer in the image of the young woman is real, and only with her own shamed goodness can she crawl from this morass.

Jesus' Daughter depicts a woman's struggle to come to terms with the actions of a sexually abusive father who denies the abuse ever took place. A little girl is raped by her father and is triggered into remembering the repeated violations in her adult life, but the father denies all and the mother ignores that this has happened. What can be believed is only what has not been disproved. That which has not yet fallen victim to being exposed is thus still vulnerable to humanity's inability to understand completely anything around it. Who is telling the truth? Which mask is real? As you come to believe a mask, it is removed and you know the face below is genuine, only to have it removed and reveal the true face beneath it. Is this last disclosure the reality or have we just stopped removing masks?

Who is to be believed when a woman's body remembers fragmented and traumatic events from childhood, events not so focused, but actions in the form of body reflexes and shadows in the mind? Whose truth do we consider, the dramatic protestations of the accused or the wounded plea of the woman child? The mother, the only person who can rescue the daughter, is passive. Yet her reticence is an active abandonment of the daughter. She too often is willing to sacrifice her daughter to save herself. We stand in horror at what can be done to young children, who are left forever fragmented. If we were able to follow the hidden threads back from the wounded adult to the besieged child, we would know life's realities, but how truthful are the memories buried in our bodies and acted out as improper behavior triggered by these lost events? That women and children are abused and that this is intolerable finds no argument. The dancer in *Jesus' Daughter* is placed in a virtual video environment at the beginning of the opera. She is clearly in despair, but we are not sure why. Her movements control the computer video presentation like a conduit from the inner soul of the young woman, allowing us to see in non-cognitive ways the unshaped horrors. This tragic scene ends without resolution with a naive madrigal in celebration of the innocence of young ladies. Without comment, the abuse that we witnessed is set aside as if it did not occur. This story is about a twentieth-century malfunction, "the American version of the Holocaust." This is a modern morality play, where god is dead but evil is alive. This is the modern tragedy, magnified and isolated.

Jesus' Daughter moves beyond formal concerns and enters the social and political sphere. The true story is charged with social commentary, guiding and provoking viewers to observe and question the world around them. The technology becomes a vehicle to communicate powerfully about the world around them. The opera, on one level, is about a specific violence and violation. But on another level it is a compelling drama that plunges headlong into the psychology of unempowerment and the journey to reclaiming power by an individual. This young woman gives to all of us a pathway to healing within ourselves as she embarks upon a virtual journey toward the regeneration of the soul. Technology is used as a transparent vehicle to explore our ability to perceive truth in a chaotic world and question institutional forces that govern how we judge truth as a society.

The final redemption is the regeneration of the soul and the reclaiming of one's life, whether it is by a nation or by an individual. Universally, it is about the misuse of power at any cost. The ability to overcome this abuse against all odds becomes the bequest to oneself and to the next generation.

Jesus' Daughter crosses boundaries in terms of art and social issues. This is not a boundary to be taken lightly, nor does this work do so.

Art is a too-little-used conduit to the soul. It can be a gift from the artist to the wounded, a gift that provides a path to healing in ways that traditional therapy cannot provide. It stands as a beacon to the heart and a salve for inner feelings. Art does not arbitrarily stand back from judging. It does not have the luxury of being objective or legally just. It sees events through specially coated lenses. It is not that art is truth, but often it is the only truth.

Note

1. Sandra L. Bloom, M.D., Medical Director, *Sanctuary* Northwestern Institute.

7

SIMPLE MINDS, COMPLEX DISTINCTIONS:
READING *FORREST GUMP* AND *PLEASANTVILLE*
THROUGH THE LENS OF BOURDIEU'S SOCIOLOGICAL THEORY

Patricia Reynaud

For the last twelve years I have been teaching seminars on the Sociology of French Culture using Pierre Bourdieu's texts as my primary reference material. My writing has been strongly informed by his theories and his developments of field, habitus and legitimacy. A few years ago I presented a paper on film studies in a panel focusing on Memory and Representation. The film *Forrest Gump* was my subject. This choice was grounded on what I perceived as the film's problematic treatment of forty years of American history, from the 1950s to the1980s. The erasure of historical relevance and the significance of this erasure prompted my analysis using Bourdieu's theories of cultural production and their imbeddedness in historicity. In other words, the film's representation of historical events serves to distort cultural memory, and the misrepresentation of interpersonal dynamics reinforces naive social conventions.

The implications of the sociologist's basic definition of a social space as a field of objective relations between positions occupied by social agents was the point of departure of my analysis of the film. Indeed any social space, be it fictional or real, implies a hierarchy in the classification of agents, a kind of "dominant-dominated" relationship. But, in odd ways, the film resisted the domination theory while submitting to it with unashamed and naive systematicity. For, how could a dominated agent like Gump possibly become dominant while managing to bypass the required steps ensuring a sucessful domination? The film provides the viewer with a simplistic recipe for success, one which maintains purity of heart and decency of motives. A film being a fictional construct, perhaps the intention of the director was not to inscribe the portrayal of social antagonisms. This fact acknowledged, the film is deceptive because these antagonisms pervade the narrative from beginning to end, climaxing with the Vietnam War.

The social and historical transparency serves as a background through which the hero walks, acts, and creates to realize his true nature, thus reinforcing an innocent view of the strength of American individualism. This view goes against the grain of a conception of the social realm as inescapable. It was also rendering unproblematic the notion of historicity of events in which culture is inscribed: Forrest is not changed by the events he witnesses even when directly involved in them. Another more recent film, *Pleasantville,* can be discussed as a healthy complement and a needed remedial context for the first film. *Pleasantville* affords the further development of the argument that, as individuals, we are not passive recipients of historical contingency but the makers of our culture, since we participate in its creation and in the changeability of things.

In this discussion, my primary focus will be on legitimation. Bourdieu's concept of legitimacy helps articulate the notions "field" and "habitus," since what is legitimate is that which is recognized by the dominant agents in a given field (be it art, politics, sports, religion, business), as well as that which is accepted and valorized as rules of conduct by each agent. In the literary field, for example, legitimate works are consecrated generally in one of two ways: through the distribution of literary prizes such as the coveted Goncourt in France or Pulitzer in the United States on the one hand, or institutionally, through their appearance on university reading lists, on the other. Legitimacy is a tacit acknowledgment among the dominant, serving to exclude the dominated. The latter, as they try to imitate the dominant, become oppressed by a value system that will never be theirs. They therefore participate in the reinforcement of their own domination. Legitimacy is to exclusion what meritocracy is to integration.

Legitimation might best be understood by analyzing its counterpart, subversion. New agents or dominated agents in a field often seek to legitimize unrecognized works as part of a strategy to subvert the system and thereby dominate the new order. To use Bourdieu's theory in a literature class, for example, can be read as an act of subversion whose aim is to legitimize new ways of looking at literature as well as legitimizing those agents capable of pursuing such activities.[1] Legitimacy is part of a continuous struggle for domination that often reflects generational conflicts. Dominant agents have an interest in preserving the status quo while the dominated, who would like to be dominators, often strive to subvert it.

Bourdieu analyzes how, in the context of nineteenth-century French literature, the poet Charles-Pierre Baudelaire and the writer Gustave Flaubert are pioneers, in that they enable the field to evolve toward a pure and disinterested vision, a vision divorced from outcome, a vision of Art for Art's sake. This vision is realized by the perfection of the formal quality of their writing as opposed to the content of the bourgeois novel, with its acquiescence to money, honors, and success. However, this disinterested vision can be regarded as a new investment that in no way compromises the status of the writer, whose only renewed interest is to bet on aloofness from practical and money concerns. Flaubert, especially, managed to create a new legitimacy based on despising the bourgeoisie. However, this elitism was unconsciously born from the resentment of being a relatively poor member of the bourgeois class.

Legitimation entails symbolic violence. There is absolutely no need to resort to brute force in order for legitimacy to impose itself and be maintained over time. On the contrary, the concept of symbolic violence ensures coherency and reproduction of an order based on exclusion. One can call it "la manière douce" (the soft way), a form of seductive practice that condemns victims to no other choice but to accept their own submission. Symbolic violence operates by manipulating the reality of social relations and entails the willful participation of the so-called victims. This manipulation of the positional relationships to establish a superiority, a position of dominance, and finally a place to project exclusion ensures symbolic violence. If one substitutes the playful notion of "finesse," this manipulation is especially relevant to "democratic" societies where the use of force has supposedly disappeared. But it is a type of violence, of the worst kind perhaps, since it acts upon the mind, a psychological violence, which, legitimized, represents a convenient way for the dominants to justify their domination while those who are excluded blame themselves for their inadequacy or incompetency.

For Flaubert, this notion amounts to denigrating the literature of his predecessors, be it bourgeois cultural production and its commercial art in need of a large public, or social art (i.e., moralizing art) fashionable among realist writers. Flaubert negates both positions in the literary field, a refusal that can also be interpreted as a choice for a philosophy of indetermination. According to Bourdieu, this position (or lack thereof) is illusory since no agent can ever escape his/her inscription in the social space. Flaubert, like the characters he portrays in his novels, brackets the illusio[2] characteristic of any field. He does not invest himself in the social game because he is unable to take seriously the stakes of the games called "serious."

A field that Bourdieu qualifies as autonomous, the literary domain is, after Flaubert, constituted as an independent world, disinterested, directly opposed to money, to compromises from the socioeconomic world, to power and market. The bohemian artists had, even before 1848, criticized the conventionality of the official artists, thus making the point that one can defy social hierarchy and be close to the commoner through a chosen poverty and yet be separated from the same commoner by an aristocratic lifestyle, prone to adopt any form of cultural transgression as long as it is opposed to cultural norms.

This world is thus its own market: one is read and appreciated by other artists, a world directly opposed to the bourgeois universe and literature, considered as a debased cultural production of upstarts without culture. The autonomous field creates its own grounds for legitimacy, not the least of which is the radical break it makes with the dominant. The new cursed artist, under the sign of its future recognition, bypasses the problematic of power which defines all social relationships in the field of cultural production. As expected, Bourdieu accuses Flaubert of unconscious aristocratic views.

Only in appearance is the realist field endowed with the same sense of radicalness. In truth, its moralism hides a disguised conformity. Flaubert's detachment, on the other hand, breaks away from any ethical affinity with the political regime. He creates his position in the field by inscribing it against those already established. His distancing from all institutions seeks to define an inverted law of supply and demand, or an inverted economic world: the artist's triumph requires his losing in the economic sphere. Flaubert's position as a person of private means facilitates tremendously the success of his endeavor.

The notion of impassibility (synonymous with passive resistance or resistance through writing) praised by Flaubert is explained as a disguised strategy of distinction, the triviality of the contents being only important in the form of the writing. Flaubert appropriates the project of his adversaries, the realists, and redefines it against them; his writings have "style" but prove nothing. Any social reality is only written to be constituted aesthetically. Flaubert's pure vision is accomplished by being equally distant from all positions in the literary field. The moving effects of the impartial description of human misery, for example, are best achieved in the short story "A Simple Heart," as the reader is able to conceive of the sanctity of the heroine, Felicité, despite the trivial character of the theme.

Forrest Gump *and* Pleasantville

Forrest Gump[3] is also the story of a simple heart, produced one century later and in another country. I will discuss the film in the context of Bourdieu's theory and show that his concepts are also useful for analyzing American popular culture. Gump's "habitus" is that of a relatively dominated agent. His mother owns a boardinghouse in the rural South, a culturally dominated part of the country. Furthermore, the hero is atypical in that his IQ is below average.[4] He is therefore dominated with respect to the cultural capital available to him (which also includes his geographic origin), the economic capital owned by his family, and the lack of social capital, as he is not part of a network of relations which could help him to establish himself. As if these were not enough, he is also physically handicapped as a child. The point that all odds are against him is well proven. Being a lonely character, he does not have friends except for one dominated like himself, his sweetheart, Jenny. His habitus is surprisingly stable and his eventual material success does not change him, nor does it alter his integrity. He remains the simple, honest, innocent Forrest Gump of the beginning of the movie. He is no doubt slow-minded, a flaw that accounts for his being perceived as socially stupid perhaps, because, by not being the least bit suspicious, he takes everybody at face value. In short, he sets himself apart from the American paranoia of being taken advantage of.

The stability of his habitus conjures up the notion of "impassibility," already discussed as part of Flaubert's required ethical conduct. While the notion was, in Flaubert's case, used as a means of distinction, in the film it connotes a reductive stand: an impassibility in the face of adversity as a kind of attitude of acceptance of what is and what happens, linked with a refusal to bear judgment on what people are, what they do, and why they are a certain way. There is no need for Forrest to adapt; he only has to remain his true self. Actually, those who adapt, change, become "street-wise" are destroyed for making errors in decisions. For instance, Jenny makes mistakes about man's nature because she keeps re-creating the abused situation she suffered in her past. Furthermore, while Flaubert's impassibility was translated into an aesthetically pleasing and prolific prose, Forrest's impassibility consists mostly of silences.[5] If, the saying goes, "talk is silver but silence is gold," then silences, as the film ultimately points out, may be the best strategy in a situation of socially conflicting interests.[6]

In sociological terms, Gump experiences an ascending social trajectory, succeeds beyond all hopes in the various fields in which he finds himself involved: sports, army, business.[7] What was necessary for Flaubert, to locate himself against the various positions in the literary field, is irrelevant to Gump. The basic opposition existing in Flaubert's time between culture and money (having one usually meant lacking the other) is no longer operational in the film and has to be reformulated. To be subservient to authorities, as the army episode in the film shows, is what pays in the end. It has long been a topos to say that American society is consensual and French society antagonistic. These simplistic binary oppositions function marvelously in the film. Also, good fortune has to be part of the divine plan, and Forrest is naturally able to find himself at the right place at the right time. The shrimp business (as well as the providential storm) which launches his fortune and bankrupts his competitors is indicative of the fact that events happen to him more than he makes them happen. In this sense, the film goes against the grain of the myth of the self-made man who, more often than not, is portrayed as a workaholic. But, in odd ways, it verifies the (modified) formula "when there is a (good) will, there is a (good) way." Higher goals concur to make him wealthy, goals that I will qualify as "secular salvation," an oxymoron perhaps, representing the category opposed to money in an American context.[8]

As for legitimacy, it is also subject to an interesting twist. Usually, the concept means a tacit agreement among dominants to exclude those who are dominated. Here legitimacy and meritocracy conflate: Forrest Gump is admitted into the dominant circles and, despite his incongruous behavior, he manages to be, if not accepted, at least tolerated. The episode of his meeting with presidents (Johnson then Kennedy) proves this eloquently. Being endowed with the right type of values, being a war hero, pays off even if it is not clear what Gump's own viewpoint is on the legitimacy of war.

The film replicates Flaubert's problematic of noncommitment. In Vietnam, Forrest is the perfect soldier, obedient and brave. When he has an opportunity to specify his position on the war issue, at a subsequent peace demonstration in Washington, D.C., microphones are disconnected to prevent him from speaking and his discourse remains, like his life, a blank episode. The paradoxical attitudes with respect to noncommitment are, in the end, opposed. Flaubert opts for high culture, since any social reality is a distraction from a superior reality, the superiority of style, whereas the movie director chooses a popular culture medium to point out that commitment is not an essential component of social reality in which whatever happens happens. This is the reason why Flaubert disdained to take part, or take sides, in the 1848 revolution. To the contrary, Forrest Gump is a good citizen, prone to accept his civic duty. However, the critical "reading" is ambiguous since he is allied with neither the views of the pro-war faction nor those of peace activists. Gump only serves and does not seek any glory from his service. His involvement seems to be made more by default than because of an ideological standpoint. Never is the status quo of the establishment criticized directly or indirectly by the character or by the director. The underlying structure purports that things are in order because they are in the order of things (what is called doxa), and this statement goes far beyond the point of view from which the film is narrated, that is, a simple mind.

This lack of questioning refers precisely to "symbolic violence." For a single idealized Forrest Gump, there are many losers in the film, victims of ideological fads: his girlfriend is first a victim of abuse then AIDS; Bubba, his African-American friend in Vietnam, loses his life, while his Lieutenant Dan keeps his, but returns crippled. If Lieutenant Dan achieves a radical transformation, it is out of despair more than out of a conviction about the tragedy of wars which only serve the political interests of the dominant. Failure happens by being too attached to causes or things. On the contrary, Forrest Gump takes no stand on anything but retains his honesty and child-like nature. This is why, formally speaking, although the historical context of the film covers events important to American society (between 1950 and 1980), they are but ripples on the surface of the hero's mind. His brain registers these events, does not judge them, and lets them go. Life goes on, always changing. Forrest is the only invariant in this turmoil.[9] Faithful to his friend Dan and to his girlfriend who finally becomes his wife, he, at the end, finds a real companion in his son. All through these years, he is there for others as his mother was for him.

If material failure is not a sign of stupidity for Flaubert but one of distinction, academic intelligence, in the film, is not a prerequisite for success. Does it exemplify the parable that the last ones can be first as early as in their earthly existence if their intentions are pure? Then money is the reward and secular salvation[10] is achieved. Or does it hint at a much more subtle interpretation, questioning altogether the concept of legitimacy as erroneous, due to its divisiveness, since Forrest's attitude results in circumventing the logic of legitimacy by not buying into it? Then, the happy outcome is thwarted by the initial premise and not by an act of will, as he does not buy into it because he is too dumb to do so. Cynicism and skepticism, the very concepts that anchored Flaubert in the conviction that no position whatsoever in the social space is worth fighting for, and, *a fortiori,* dying for, have no room in the movie. As for Bourdieu, he explains his position on the relativity of values which are not universal and are inscribed in history. Only education enables us to act upon them.[11] In the film, scholastic achievement is discarded as unneccessary because these values cannot really be acted upon.

The attitude of the anti-hero seems, finally, the wisest one: he does not make mistakes because he is never bound by his allegiances. For example, despite his love for Jenny, he never forces her to stay with him. She is the one who chooses to come back to him at the end. Furthermore, his subservient nature could be the necessary quality for a free spirit, which subscribes to nonattachment, and whose honesty goes beyond a mere facade. Forest Gump is truly respectful of others, independently of their sex, ethnic background, or social status.

Cultural differences are indeed ingrained in us through our habitus. Perhaps because I am from Europe, I too, after seeing its redeeming qualities, read this film as a terribly individualistic[12] and superficial narrative: I strongly share Bourdieu's opinions that it is possible, thanks to education and culture, to modify relations of power constitutive of any social space. Denying it is to succumb to fate, and fate is, to say the least, unpredictable. The film is as good at evading sociopolitical issues as Gump is at trivializing or at least simplifying moral issues: as a child, he perceives them as good or bad.

The movie teases us by raising but not resolving moral and social questions, questions such as: why is Gump, an idiot, made successful? Should all idiots enjoy success? Is radical innocence[13] the saving grace of stupidity? Are the two even connected? There is some truth in Flaubert's statement that "stupidity rests on concluding," a phrase which fits the deconstructionist vein of our time perfectly. But as Flaubert refuses to conclude because his encyclopedic mind knows too much, Forrest manages not to conclude because of his simple-mindedness. As his mother used to put it in a language meaningful to him (and vacuous to others): "Life is a box of chocolates; you never know what you'll get."

There is another box in the film: the television set. Toward the end of the film, Forrest's way of bonding with his young son is to watch television. Another film, *Pleasantville,* directed by Gary Ross and released in 1998, starts with a quite naive adolescent hero, David, mesmerized by the screen where his favorite show, *Pleasantville Marathon,* is taking place. This later film seems to offer a perfect complement to *Forrest Gump* in that it answers some of the puzzling questions raised in the former. It is also a retrospective of the fifties. On the surface of events, everything is pleasant in "Pleasantville," an ideal place where things are as they ought to be. David knows everything about the various episodes in the show he watches; he has memorized all the lines and is able to answer any question about the characters, their lives, relationships, and whereabouts. David seems amused and perhaps a bit nostalgic about those good old fifties values where men are socially dominant and women seem happy to perform the household chores. The motto "Honey, I'm home" triggers the same reaction in each episode: the dutiful wife, neatly dressed and made up, appears to greet her husband who is ready after a day of work for a substantial dinner cooked with love. If nostalgia is there, it may in part come from the fact that David tries to find some solace from a rather dysfunctional family and a divorced and terribly depressed mother.

But the passive viewing is soon to end: David, far from being an obedient spectator, becomes actively involved in the "rewriting" of the script of the Pleasantville saga. Such a rewriting would delight Flaubert because art will play a major part in the new script and it would also please Bourdieu in that the notions of diversity, exclusion, and domination will be also added to fit the politically correct discourse of the nineties. The television repairman acts as a "deus ex machina" who enables David and his sister Jennifer to make the jump into the television set and become part of the making of the show, in so doing changing identity and becoming Bud and Mary Sue. It helps to enter the world of the fifties having the knowledge of the nineties, in that it creates a historical perspective lacking in *Forrest Gump.*

With the first reaction of surprise behind them, Bud is eager to remain in his favorite show, to play by the rules and not to deviate one bit from his set knowledge, thereby respecting the script to the letter. But his sister is less willing to commit herself to her new role, for obvious reasons, and demands to return home immediately. But as the new script is rewritten, Mary Sue dares to ask the questions that no one asked before. She is the initiator of change, the initiator of men's sexual advances. She introduces her mother to sexual pleasure by explaining to her what it is all about. Time and again, the movie emphasizes how young women initiate and benefit from social change, whereas men have a vested interest in preserving a status quo which serves them quite well in terms of privileges, not the least being symbolic. The few men willing to try something new, such as Bill the fast food waiter, are at the bottom of the social scale and/or have unfulfilled desires. For example, Bill dreams of becoming an artist.

From a visual perspective, each change in *Pleasantville* adds colors on the screen as well as social diversity of thoughts, words, and actions. From a pasty black-and-white film, bathed in historical flatness, the movie evolves to a visual delight of art and colors which ruptures the sense of conformity and isolation. White rural/suburban middle-class America gives way to alternative lifestyles and a nonconsensual society which finally has to deal with historical relevance. This presents a coping mechanism that *Forrest Gump* was unable to provide, since the point of that movie was not to make anyone think.[14]

In the first film, history is devoid of cultural significance as no real change impacts on the main character. In the second film, change is not only acceptable and desirable but inevitable. The lesson presented is that the potential for evolution is already in oneself. Indeed the social circumstances of our lives are the vehicle for individual transformation and the cumulation of these changes results in new cultural contexts. To understand modern culture requires an understanding of social dynamics in terms of its conflictual potentials.

The indeterminacy in the endings of these two films is of starkly different character. Forrest does not change through his historical journey. In *Pleasantville,* the mother is uncertain as to whether she will stay with her husband or join her lover Bill, now a painter. There is no right or wrong answer; there is only historical significance, onto which events are recorded, values are erected, and roles are inscribed in a context of constant evolution. And the naively personalistic vision of the singularity of individuals is to be reassessed taking into account social structures, because the individual speaks his truth through these structures.

Notes

1. The notion of subversion renders appropriate a comparison between Flaubert and Bourdieu. The true sociologist has always aspired to be a true iconoclast. Like Flaubert in literature, Bourdieu is at the periphery of sociology in France. His position within the academic field is problematic, notwithstanding the fact that Bourdieu does have symbolic power.

2. Literary illusio is for the writer or reader to adhere to the literary game, that is, to believe that the game is important and that it conditions aesthetic pleasure. It means to participate fully in the fictional game and to agree fully with the presuppositions of the world of fiction. That is why Madame Bovary, as a character, is so enmeshed in the fictional novels she reads that she really lives out the fictional clichés as the myth of pure love. The result is obviously disillusion, for she cannot implicate herself in the dull reality around her. Reality is also based on an illusio, but of another kind. While the literary illusio is reserved to the happy few and is the privilege of those who are able to spend their life pursuing a literary adventure, it is opposed to the banal illusio, the one most shared by humankind, the illusio of common sense. The field of literature or science is opposed to common sense, that is, to a doxic adhesion to the ordinary world.

3. Directed by Robert Zemeckis (*Back to the Future*) and winner of several Academy Awards: best actor, best picture, and best director in 1994.

4. I am referring to an atypicality in the common portrayal of film heroes. Culturally, Gump may represent a typical stereotype of a white male living in the rural South, as is portrayed in films such as *Deliverance* (directed by John Boorman) and *Shy People* (directed by Andrei Konchelovsky).

5. One can interpret silences as an easy way to evade issues raised by the film, issues such as war, corruption in politics, romantic love, sports, and the place of money. These silences point to the exact opposite of an iconoclastic and/or subversive attitude. Other more problematic films also feature a mentally

deficient person as their central character, such as *Being There* (a Peter Sellers film directed by Hal Ashby) and *Rain Man* (1989, directed by Barry Levinson). In *Being There* the protagonist, a gardener, speaks only garden terminology and his discourses are interpreted by the body politic as metaphors for highly profound statements. Only one person is not fooled by words, the gardener himself, James, since he takes them at face value!

6. In no way do I mean to silence Forrest's voice as he narrates the story of his life to the occasional listeners who are also waiting for the bus. They are fortuitous characters, seated next to him by chance. Forrest seems to tell his autobiography to himself or to us, the audience.

7. He starts as a football star then becomes a war hero and a Ping-Pong champ, then finds success as a shrimp boat captain. At last the money from his corporation is safely invested by his friend and first mate Dan (his former lieutenant) and he does not need to work any longer.

8. Forrest has strong, although simplistic, religious convictions. Having listened to his mother, who, interestingly enough, is the only person he understands, he has also retained what she imparted to him. It must have been his destiny to become rich "unless it was floating around, or both at the same time," he says toward the end of the movie in an obviously inconclusive fashion.

9. Peter Rose, classics professor at Miami University, commented on a local radio program (April 13, 1995): "The history of our times—the Vietnam War, a string of utterly corrupt presidents, movements for social change—a history of which he is the utterly unreflective witness and in which he is the meaningless participant—*history* in this vision emerges as a sequence of sight gags. In short, *Forrest Gump* represents the ideal consequences of the Republican assault on education."

10. It thus appears to give credit to the belief in the healing power of love. On a symbolic level, however, when there is healing, there has to be self-transformation, a transformation absent in the film in the same way that knowledge is absent. This relates to the point made by Rose (in note 9). The movie provides for neither alternative.

11. The film does not reconcile any opposition between being inspired by the character or knowing about him since there is nothing to know. There is no knowledge as well as no hope, in the sense of secular imagination.

12. Individualistic because social antagonisms are depoliticized, thus imposing new and subtle forms of subordination (to destiny, for example) rather than fostering true individual respect.

13. "Radical innocence" is not used here to refer to the English romantic notion of nineteenth-century literature but more to the twentieth-century American ideal of "rags to riches" as the archetype of the one who, because he is virtuous, finally wins. Many fairy tales recount this theme that seems to refer to yet another myth of American culture.

14. The episode in question occurs when the male establishment of Pleasantville becomes horrified when one of its members shows the sign of distraction and moral decay via the inscription on his shirt which his wife burnt into it while ironing it. When the husband requests an explanation, his wife replies that she "was thinking. . . ."

Works Cited

Bourdieu, Pierre. 1977. *Outline of a Theory of Practice*. Trans. Richard Nice. Cambridge: Cambridge UP.

——. 1984. *Distinction: A Social Critique of the Judgement of Taste*. Trans. Richard Nice. Cambridge: Harvard UP.

——. 1996. *Rules of Art: Genesis and Structure of the Literary Field*. Trans. Susan Emanuel. Palo Alto, CA: Stanford UP.

Bourdieu, Pierre, and Loïc Wacquant. 1992. *An Invitation to Reflexive Sociology*. Chicago: U of Chicago P.

8

SPECTACULAR SUFFERING:
PERFORMING PRESENCE, ABSENCE, AND WITNESS
AT U.S. HOLOCAUST MUSEUMS

Vivian Patraka

No historical referent is stable, transparent in its meaning, agreed upon in its usage, or even engaged with in the same way by any large group of people.[1] One way of contextualizing the current movement of the term Holocaust is by invoking Michel de Certeau's distinction (1984) between a place and a space in his application of spatial terms to narrative. For de Certeau, the opposition between "place" and "space" refers to "two sorts of stories" or narratives about how meaning is made. Place refers to those operations that make its object ultimately reducible to a fixed location, "to the *being there* of something dead, [and to] the law of a place" where the stable and "the law of the 'proper'" rules. Place "excludes the possibility of two things being in the same location. . . . Space occurs as the effect produced by the operations that orient it, situate it, temporalize it, and make it function in a polyvalent way." Thus space is created "by the actions of historical *subjects*." These actions multiply spaces and what can be positioned within them. Finally, the relation between place and space is a process whereby "stories thus carry out a labor that constantly transforms places into spaces or spaces into places" (117-18). De Certeau's distinction between a place and a space is crucial to my argument in the way it clarifies the differing strategies of attempting to move people through a landscape whose meanings are uniquely determined in contrast to providing an opportunity for contestation and multiplicity of association.

I want to employ this distinction between place and space in considering how the referent of the Holocaust is configured by contemporary American Jews.[2] Indeed, for generations of American Jews born in the

---

Reprinted from chapter 6 of Patraka's *Spectacular Suffering: Theater, Fascism, and the Holocaust* (1999), with the permission of Indiana University Press.

1940s and after, it can be said that the Holocaust is constitutive of our "Jewishness" itself, sometimes operating at the expense of other Jewish traditions and histories. So despite the very palpable differences among us, both culturally and politically, it is still the case that many of our responses to the images, objects, and words connected to the Holocaust are "hard-wired," provoking automatic emotional meanings and an attitude of reverence. This widespread response makes it hard to get beyond a consensus on the agony, the loss, and the mindful viciousness that produced them so we can discern the actual discourse generated about the Holocaust and how it functions. Some of the strategies of this discourse are manipulative; they solicit our anguish, horror, and fear as the grounds for asserting larger meanings to which we may not wish to assent. But neither avoidance of the places in which these "fixed" narratives reside nor simple dismissal is, I think, useful. For this would risk separating us from our own emotions about the Holocaust, entombing them in these monumental stories so that they are no longer available for either examination or change. Instead, we have to create spaces for critique within and among those seemingly inevitable emotional hard-wirings and the places to which they get connected.

The following discussion is a step in that direction. I explore how the referent of the Holocaust is configured at sites in the United States where a cultural performance of Holocaust history is being staged for public consumption—the U.S. Holocaust Memorial Museum in Washington, D.C., and the Beit Hashoah Museum of Tolerance in Los Angeles. My purpose in doing so is to honor this history, but also to renegotiate its effects by rethinking the set of practices set up by these two important museums for the sake of both the present and the future. I also want to view each of the museums against the background of their mass-mailed fund-raising letters to explore some of their ideological underpinnings. Finally, my intent in the discussion that follows is to enact a performative, de Certeauian space by not fixing the museums in advance within particular Holocaust narratives, so I can continue a process of discovery for both myself and my readers.

The fund-raising letters of both museums claim the term Holocaust in its Jewish specificity by enlarging its applications to include or relate to other oppressed groups. Both articulate the United States to genocide, but in contrasting ways: the D.C. letters locate the United States as a site of release from genocide;[3] the L.A. letters configure the United States as a potential site for genocide. Finally, the announcements of both museums reveal how each museum, perhaps inevitably, given the desire to memorialize, oscillates between space and place—between the desire to provide spaces where museum-goers can perform acts of reinterpretation as historical subjects and the need to insist on the more public modality of inscribing over and over on a more passive audience the logic of a place conveying the monumental meaning of the Holocaust.

The U.S. Holocaust Memorial Museum:
Narratives of Liberation and Democracy

We had downstairs [in the museum] waiting in line a lady being asked by a little child, what is the difference between freedom and liberated? And the mother, I couldn't butt into the middle, couldn't give that child the difference. But when you say liberated, you have to be enslaved first in order to be liberated, but freedom doesn't matter, wherever you are you can be free.

—Mr. Harold Zissman, member of the Jewish resistance and survivor of the Holocaust, spoken to the author at the U.S. Holocaust Memorial Museum, 1993

In order to elicit donations, the fund-raising materials for the U.S. Holocaust Memorial Museum in Washington, D.C., indicate what the museum promises to accomplish—a self-presentation that represents the main thrust of this institution (Bal 1992, 558) and prefigures many of the strategies designed for the museum itself. I believe the target audience for these fund-raising letters is, primarily, the American Jewish community, while the letters identify the target spectatorship for the museum as the public at large. A captioned photograph locates the museum by its proximity to the Washington Monument as a means of validating it spatially as a national project. Quotations by Presidents Carter, Reagan, and Bush about the Holocaust further authenticate this undertaking, along with a 1945 statement by Eisenhower—not as president, but as general and liberator—asserting that he could give "firsthand evidence" of the horrors he saw "if ever there develops a tendency to charge these allegations merely to 'propaganda.'" Also included on the flyer is an official-looking image of the 1980 Public Law to create an independent federal establishment that will house "a permanent living memorial museum to the victims of the Holocaust" ("a short walk from our great national memorials" and hence, implicitly, connected to them). The effect of this link is deliberately to blur the boundaries between the privately sponsored and the governmentally mandated as a way to inscribe the museum as much as possible within the legitimizing discourse of its host country.[4]

Of course, any Holocaust Museum must enter into a dialogue with the country in which it is located and with the positioning of that country in Holocaust events, but the D.C. museum's emphasis on its geographies of announcement is insistent. A clear anxiety about denials of both the events of the Holocaust and its moral significance for Americans is embedded in these recurrent claims for legitimacy, even if some of the hyperbolic language can be chalked up to the discourse of fund-raising, which in itself constitutes a kind of melodrama of persuasion. Inevitably, an American Holocaust museum is caught on the cusp of happened here/happened there, a conundrum, as James Young formulated it (1992), over whether American history means events happening here or the histories Americans carry with them. But given the large proportion of Jews living in America compared to Europe, this museum has a context of survival, of a "living memorial" *by* the living (as framers, funders, visitors) that those in the devastated landscape of Europe can never possess. This, too, is part of American history.

Presumably, then, learning about the events of the Holocaust, *precisely* because they didn't happen here, creates what one newsletter calls a "meaningful testament" to the values and ideals of democracy, thereby inscribing the museum within the history of American democracy and our rituals of consensus about what that democracy means, if not within American history per se. It could be argued, then, that in this museum the Constitution is to be viewed through the prism of Jewish history as much as Jewish history is to be viewed through the prism of the Constitution. Thus one of the central strategies of the museum is to assert the way in which American mechanisms of liberal democratic government would prevent such a genocidal action from occurring in the United States, as well as partially to overlap, for the U.S. viewer, the perspective of the victims of genocide with that of the victors of World War II. This latter aspect would enhance what Philip Gourevitch (1993) describes as the museum's project to reinforce "the ethical ideals of American political culture by presenting the negation of those ideals" as well as our historical response to them (55). In fact, images of American troops liberating the concentration camps constitute part of the final exhibit of the museum as well as the opening tactic of the Holocaust exhibit proper, where all that is seen and heard is presented through the eyes and ears of the liberating soldiers. Even the survivor testimony played for us in an amphitheater at the end of the exhibit prominently includes one narrative by a Holocaust survivor who eventually married the soldier who liberated her. Indeed, this marriage emplotment seems to embody a crucial strategy of the whole museum, with Jews and Jewish history (the feminized victim) married to American democracy (the masculinized liberator). Recalling that the American liberator in this survivor testimony is Jewish as well, I must note another, more implicit enactment in the museum, that of consolidating an American Jewish identity by marrying the positions of liberator and victim.

If what is critical for the museum's project is to extend our fictions of nationhood by the premise that a democratic state comes to the aid of those peoples outside its borders subjected to genocide, then the conferring of liberation becomes the story of American democracy. To assert this story entails backgrounding the masses of people who died before liberation (as opposed to the pitiful remnant left). It entails foregrounding the assumption that waging war can actually accomplish something and, more precisely, that saving Jews, Gypsies, leftists, Catholic dissenters, homosexuals, and Polish forced labor from the Nazis was one of the goals of World War II, rather than a byproduct of winning the war by invading the enemies' territory. I could dismiss the museum's overall strategy as a simplistic appeal to hegemonic structures of governance. But to do so would be to deny that the museum *must engage* U.S. viewers with an ethical narrative of national identity in direct relation to the Holocaust. The alternative is to risk becoming a site for viewing the travails of the exoticized Other from elsewhere ("once upon a time"), or, even worse, "a museum of natural history for an endangered species" (Bal 1992, 560).

Moreover, the museum itself does not produce this idea of liberation from genocide as a completely unproblematic and unquestioned historical reality. Within the physical and conceptual envelope of its democratic discourse, the museum offers viewers a display of documents that echo and summarize parts of David Wyman's examination (1984) of "the abandonment of the Jews" by the U.S. government. The museum displays the actual telegrams that communicate how, as late as February of 1943, with the "final solution" fully operational in European death camps, the State Department tried to shut down the channel for receiving information about what was happening to European Jews (information also designated for delivery via the State Department to the Jewish-American community). The rationale was that such information would compromise our relations with the neutral countries from which these secret communications were emanating (Berenbaum 1993, 161-64). This policy of suppression of information about and denial of aid to European Jews was challenged only by the intense labor of several men in the Treasury Department who had secretly learned of the State Department's policy. Their efforts finally culminated in Randolph Paul's January 1944 "Report to the Secretary [of the Treasury] on the Acquiescence of This Government in the Murder of the Jews." To make a long, painful story short, in January 1944, Secretary of the Treasury Henry Morgenthau took this information to Franklin Delano Roosevelt, persuading him to establish the War Refugee Board by threatening (in a presidential election year) to release documents pertaining to the government's suppression of information and assistance.

This display of information within the museum operates in an interesting way with both the museum's architecture and locale. Despite the references to its proximity to national memorials in the fund-raising materials, the museum is actually closest physically to four mundane-looking government buildings, including the Treasury Building diagonally across the street. Much has been made of the way the museum copies the blocky functionality of these buildings in its initial entranceway, because this entrance is a false one, without a roof, while the actual doors to the museum are located several feet behind it. Thus the facade of the building re-creates the solemn, neoclassical, and universalizing style of the government buildings around it, but marks its relationship to them as architecturally false. However, the documents issuing from the Treasury Building during the 1940s manifest another relationship, one based in precise historical detail, previously suppressed. This creates a chronotopic connection, that is, a scene of interaction produced simultaneously out of temporal and spatial relations between the two buildings and the histories they contain. In offering this information, the museum constructs a localized historical contradiction to its own ideological claims about how democracies respond to genocides, thereby complicating the narrative of our national identity and, in so doing, turning an ostensible narrative place into a space for negotiating meanings. Ideally, this contradiction opens a space of possibility for the spectator to consider how representative democracy operates in the present with regard to genocides elsewhere, rather than entirely soliciting a sense of disillusion, betrayal, and despair about the past.

Conversely, the fund-raising materials promise us another narrative context for making meaning out of the exhibits—one which is less palpable in the actual museum. They describe the museum's Identity Card Project, a kind of interactive theater of identification. Each museum visitor is to receive a passport-sized ID card similar to the one a victim of the Holocaust was "forced to carry in Nazi Germany." At first the card is only to show the photograph of an actual person, with a brief background; then the card can be "updated" at "regular computer stations" for a fuller account. Most interesting is the actual list of victims from which these identity cards are drawn: they include Jews, Gypsies, homosexuals, Jehovah's Witnesses, and the handicapped, as well as others the Nazis labeled "undesirables." Thus, while still emphasizing the specific reference to Jews, the canon of the Holocaust victims has been reinterpreted and expanded, most pertinently to include homosexuals, whose desire for institutionalized recognition in the past had often been met with silence or resistance. This could offer us one means of considering the relationship of Jews to Other(ed) differences.[5] Moreover, if the actual colored badges of these groups were to become part of the representation, they could convey the way the Nazis visually constructed categories of color upon religious, ethnic, sexual, political, and physical differences, thereby creating a racialized spectacle of visible difference where none existed. Such color coding could also complicate the monolith of European "whiteness" by exemplifying the ease with which that racial strategy was and continues to be manipulated for ideological and economic gain. The goal would be not to instill a passive "white terror" in white spectators, but to demonstrate the constructedness of "whiteness," its instability as a category, and the undesirability of relying on it for either self-knowledge or protection.

In the actual museum, the number of computers is inadequate to allow the enormous number of museum-goers to update their identity cards periodically, so we are simply given an identity card printed with the full individual narrative as we wait in line for the elevators to go up to the main exhibit.[6] And while the museum does exhibit multimedia materials on the persecution of Gypsies, homosexuals, and the handicapped, its documentation on the German left's treatment by the Nazis turns out to be most critical to complicating its narrative of the Holocaust for the following reason: most conventional "how did it happen" histories of the Holocaust portray an escalating narrative of obsession with, and restrictions and violence against, Jews that culminates in the "final solution." By contrast, the D.C. museum fills in some of the vacuum surrounding that history by documenting the ruthless suppression (including incarceration and murder) of Socialists and Communists from the start of the Nazi era (and early on in the exhibit, while museum-goers are still trying to read everything). This inclusion creates a fuller sense of Nazi ideology by offering the additional insight that this violence was constitutive of Nazism itself: Nazism, then, both founds itself in violence and escalates its violence in order to perpetuate itself. Including the left in this configuration also challenges the simple binary emplotment of democracy versus fascism.

However, while my readings of the actual museum emphasize sites for constructing multiple meanings and relationships, the fund-raising materials recall the larger ways in which the exhibits are to function. One flyer promises the museum will orchestrate our emotions in the mode of a spectacle designed to command attention, transfix spectators, and narrativize in advance the experience of those who approach it: "You will watch, horrified" and "you will weep" over this "heroic and tragic story." But there is also an overpowering sense of desire in all these descriptions, a need to create an utterly convincing spectacle that will say it all, stop time and space, prevent denial, and make the suffering known. Of course, no representation can do that even if we hear the "actual voices of death camp survivors tell of unspeakable horror and pain." How could the unspeakable of genocide be spoken? How could the interiority of individual suffering on a massive scale be turned inside out into an exterior, if respectful, spectacle? Perhaps this consuming desire for the real in representation, for the convincing spectacular, is inversely proportionate to the process of genocide itself, which includes the production of silence, disappearance, dispersal, and concealment as the underside of its fascistic public spectacles. Perhaps this desire responds to the fear that whatever little is left to mark it afterwards will be forgotten. Or responds to the intense anxiety created by the growing trend Deborah Lipstadt documents in *Denying the Holocaust: The Growing Assault on Truth and Memory* (1993), operating in tandem with the temporal reality that many Holocaust survivors are very old or have died, so that the live, embodied narrative that functions as a bulwark against denial is being extinguished. But the personal artifacts that the letters claim will be collected in one of the museum's rooms—the suitcases, hairbrushes, razors, photographs, diaries, dolls, toys, shoes, eyeglasses, and wedding rings—despite their vivid materiality, are finally only the small detritus of annihilation that point to the inevitable absence of complete representation.

Even the sites of artifacts whose meaning is intended to be self-evident can become spaces, instead of places, changed by the paths visitors themselves create as historical subjects. The museum went to great pains, including revising its architectural plans, to exhibit a fifteen-ton freight car used to deport Jews. Walking through it offers us a physical trace of the frightening darkness and claustrophobic agony of the one hundred people crushed into this and other such cars. But as I moved toward this train-car on the second day of my visit to the museum, I was approached by a married couple, Mrs. Sonya Zissman and Mr. Harold Zissman, who noticed I was speaking into a tape recorder and came to talk to me. Both had been involved in resistance in rural Poland and were eager to speak about this experience. They also criticized the museum for overemphasizing victimization in its portrayal of the Holocaust, while not including enough material on Jewish acts of resistance in its exhibit. Here is part of our conversation at the site of this freight car:

VP: You're survivors?
SZ: I can't look at it [the freight car], I'm sick already. My husband, he was the head of a ghetto uprising . . . it's sickening to look at. You live day and night with that, day and night, as a matter of fact we were in the underground, we [both] escaped to the underground.

VP: Were you in a particular organization, is that what made you join the underground?

SZ: Organization? Nah. We were in the ghettos. . . . We were in the Eastern part of Poland and we knew what was going on. . . . Small towns, they had wooded areas, thousands and thousands of miles with wooded areas. We ran to these areas when the killing [of Jews in the ghettos] started and this was how we survived.

HZ: I escaped the ghetto. She ran away after the massacre was taking place in her town while she was in hiding. I escaped before it started in our ghetto—and I have very bad emotions between my family who dared why I should escape [and felt betrayed and who were subsequently killed]. [He weeps.]

SZ: And then the men were forming a fighting squadron . . . and the young ones were fighting.

VP: Did you get to be part of the fighting squad?

SZ: I was. My husband was. Down there in the underground.

VP: What's it like to be in the museum today?

SZ: Horrible. I got a headache already. . . . *But we gave them hell too,* don't worry.

VP: What does that mean?

SZ: Hell. The Germans.

VP: You gave them hell? How?

SZ: We used to mine the trains that were going to the front . . . so the soldiers were going on ten, twenty—that's how long the cars, you know, and they had ammunition going there with the train and [we would] tear them apart [by planting bombs under them]. We had the Russians [helping us], in the later years, '43, I think. They used to send us down sugar and salt and what we needed for [the fighting squadron] to live on. . . . My [previous] husband, my two brothers, my mother, got killed in the ghetto. [She weeps.]

VP: How many years were you in the underground?

SZ: For three years, because as soon as the ghetto started we had an underground.

VP: You mean you two were invisible and in hiding for three years?

SZ: Of course. We had to. You had no choice.

The live performance of survivor testimony by the Zissmans, "unmanaged" as it was by the museum proper, powerfully produced me as an engaged witness to their history, forcing me to negotiate their "unofficial" story with the "official" one surrounding it. More particularly, what this conversation marked for me was how the museum's larger project of locating itself within a narrative of U.S. democracy displaced representations of acts of resistance by Jews in order to embed its narrative in the frame of American liberation (and appeal more directly to U.S. con-

sumers of museum information). Mr. Harold Zissman put it more tren-
chantly when I asked him what he thought about the exhibits:

HZ: It's not so much important what I think because we have [lived] through
that [history]. . . . We've [gone] through the ghetto part [of the museum]. Only
very few stories of our part [in this history] is being told. I wrote a scholar of
the Holocaust . . . because very little is shown about our part [i.e., the Jewish
resistance] for reasons beyond my understanding in forty some years. . . . My
own feeling is too much commercializing became the Holocaust here, the
telling about the resistance and the participation of the Jews throughout Europe
in resisting the enemy does not bring money, evidently.

VP: Victims do?

HZ: Exactly. Victims do.

Ideologically speaking, then, liberation requires a victim; there don't
have to be resisters, and it is American liberators not Jewish resisters that
"sell" the museum to the larger public in this American locale.

The Beit Hashoah Museum of Tolerance:
Narratives of Prejudice and Democracy

In the process of evaluating aspects of the U.S. Holocaust Memorial
Museum, I've asked myself, "Just what would *you* have such a museum
do? Position spectators as complicitous bystanders? As potential perpetrators of genocide? Who would come to such a museum?" The answers
to these questions are not self-evident. Locale and funding sources play a
part in shaping what a Holocaust museum shows and who sees it. That
the U.S. Holocaust Memorial Museum identifies itself as a national project imbricates the Holocaust into our national narratives, keeps a tight
focus on the history of the Holocaust, suits its Washington, D.C. locale
and its federal grant of extremely scarce land. Although the museum is
privately funded, its quasi-governmental status helps produce what is
and is not displayed within its walls.

The Beit Hashoah Museum of Tolerance is located in Los Angeles,
California, adjacent to the Simon Wiesenthal Center (to which it is orga-
nizationally connected). It was built on private land, but received consid-
erable funding from the State of California. As a result, this museum has
a more insistent emphasis on pedagogy and is more explicitly targeted
for school children and adolescents (i.e., an involuntary audience),
although claims for current technologies of representation are clearly
intended to lure the public at large and attract funding from private
donors. Under the rubric of teaching tolerance by providing examples of
intolerance, it can display injustice in the United States and include a
multiracial awareness of past and current American events. It also

responds to its more immediate locale, Los Angeles, as a site of racial and ethnic tensions, and includes those tensions (witness its speedy creation of an exhibit on the L.A. Uprising) in its exhibits. While responding to the local, the museum also locates itself as an international project that globally documents past and present violations to human rights.[7]

In accordance with these projects, the fund-raising letters sent to private donors prior to the museum's opening employ a primary strategy opposite to that of the U.S. Holocaust Memorial Museum: The Beit Hashoah Museum of Tolerance would represent the United States as a site of "bigotry and intolerance," that is, as a potential place of genocide, with the Holocaust as the most horrific illustration of where intolerance could lead. While the D.C. museum quoted U.S. presidents to authenticate its project, the Beit Hashoah's Charter Member fund-raising flyer quotes Martin Luther King, Jr.: "Like life, racial understanding is not something that we find, but something that we must create." Thus the Beit Hashoah articulates the history of the Holocaust to an American landscape of prejudice and racism, a more liberal narrative that, to some degree, troubles our sense of national identity if not, ultimately, our fundamental fictions of nationhood. Moreover, given the Beit Hashoah's claim to respond to and represent the international, the national, and the local, the focus of the museum is as diffuse (despite the presence of Holocaust exhibits that take up a fair share, but by no means most, of the museum's space and much, but not all, of the fund-raising descriptions) as the U.S. Memorial Holocaust Museum's focus is specific. This diverse range of arenas configured under the rubric of intolerance is represented in the materials that describe the path of this museum.

First, visitors are confronted by ethnic and minority stereotypes as a means to challenge their current attitudes and perceptions. Second, they enter a Tolerance Workshop where they are given an "authentic social dilemma" and asked to choose and motivate others to moral action (actually a large area resembling a video arcade where multiple interactive "games" about prejudice can be played). Third, visitors view "stereotypical ethnic and racial depictions from early movies," hear demagogues vilifying minorities, and "meet" via video "individuals who have made a difference," including Martin Luther King, Jr., Robert Kennedy, and Raoul Wallenberg. Fourth, "in a series of illuminated computer-synchronized tableaux" that are "amazingly lifelike," visitors "go back in time" to experience "the events of the Holocaust" (and Nazism). Fifth, and finally, visitors stand before a replica of the gates of Auschwitz and hear the voices of Holocaust victims speak of "suffering and heroism."

While I can appreciate the goals of a Holocaust museum that seeks to serve not only as a place to memorialize victims of persecution, but also as a laboratory for devising strategies to combat hate, violence, and prejudice in the present, I note several problems in the strategies proposed to achieve this. The continued insistence that the museum presents "real life" to viewers obscures the way it is adjusting the parameters of a discourse. Moreover, while "persecution and devastation" have been the results of both anti-Semitism and racism, the museum risks creating an abstract equivalence between the two by configuring both as "an internalized matter of prejudice" (Bourne 1987, 14). When tolerance becomes a personal matter, it cannot, for example, take into account the way racism functions as "a structural and institutional issue" within a system of power "hierarchically structured to get the maximum benefit from differentiation" (14). Showing this system of exploitative differentiation and the kinds of subject-positions it produces is especially critical for a museum about genocide: it helps bridge the gap between genocide as unthinkable (when linked to the behavior of individuals per se) and its pervasive historical reality. Moreover, discourses of various genocides themselves can be positioned as competing narratives of suffering within a system of differentiated hierarchy, resulting in what Michael Berenbaum (1990, 34) calls "a calculus of calamity." I recognize that this competitive differentiation is exactly what the Beit Hashoah Museum of Tolerance is trying to avoid, but I don't think it takes its goals far enough. And missing from the museum's landscape of intolerance are contemporary, violent outbreaks of homophobia occurring in the United States[8] as well as much mention of sexism: in practice the museum privileges racism as the site of intolerance, which is not surprising if its purpose is to forge links with other genocidal situations using the more traditional notions of "group" that govern definitions of genocide. Finally, the threat of genocide and even actions deemed potentially genocidal may not be the best measure for evaluating the everyday oppressions to which people and groups are subject, and such a treatment may even serve to minimize the importance of daily oppressions, especially when they are not in line with a teleological narrative of escalating violence.

And, despite its emphasis on the interactive, by ending with the gates of Auschwitz the museum takes the space it tries to open up for a consideration of the interconnections among oppressions and recontains it into a (computer-synchronized) place. Auschwitz becomes a monumental metonymy for the Holocaust, for all anti-Semitism(s), and for the consequences of intolerance. Using Auschwitz as an emblem for all anti-Semitism(s) may actually obscure the current mechanisms by which they function. Using Auschwitz as a metonymy for the consequences of intolerance facilitates the museum's Eurocentric gesture of locating its history of genocide only in the twentieth century. In so doing, the museum erases the historical reality that not only could genocide happen here, it *has* happened here, if not with the same obsessive deliberations associated with the "final solution." A museum with the goals of this one must take into account the massive genocidal annihilations in the Americas, and in particular, the United States, committed against indigenous peoples and against Africans during slavery.

Why doesn't it? Is showing genocide within our borders "going too far" for such a museum (while including visible timelines of other injustices to these groups is not)? More generally, should we assume that if the Jewish genocide in Europe were minimized in a site dedicated to showing intolerance, other genocides, indigenous to the United States, would inevitably become historically more visible? There are African-American and Native American museums slated for the Smithsonian Mall but, as Philip Gourevitch (1993, 62) has noted, no "Museum of Slavery" or "Trail of Tears" museum. Perhaps recognizing the contributions of specific ethnicities, emphasizing what their continuing presence and vitality offers us as a nation, constitutes a celebratory means of covering over what was done to them and who and what has been permanently lost. Our democratic discourse must repress highly visible representations of any genocide that occurred within our own national borders. Thus, in order to sustain its fictions of nationhood and its imagined community, it must produce yet another set of highly visible representations of what it marks as a genocide occurring "elsewhere." Indeed, the genocide film shown at the Beit Hashoah pertains to South American indigenous peoples, to Armenians, and to Cambodians. Curiously, then, at the Beit Hashoah, the perspective of the global with which it enhances its scope is in itself a tactful drawing of attention away from the full excess of "intolerance" in this country. From this perspective, it is the very performance of hegemonic democratic discourse, more pertinently our own "hard-wired" fictions of nationhood, that we would need to interrogate and revise in order to make genocide "at home" visible.[9]

But that still doesn't fully account for what *is* shown at the Beit Hashoah as the last big exhibit before the Holocaust wing and how it is situated: the multiscreen feature on the civil rights movement struggle, "Ain't You Gotta Right?," directed by Orlando Bagwell, who also directed the series *Eyes on the Prize*. Between the civil rights film viewing area and the Holocaust wing is a peculiar little film displaying the lives of the rich in the 1920s. It's like a sorbet, a palate cleanser between two gourmet courses. Why this rupture? Perhaps because, historically, the directional signals are different: the call for African-American civil rights is the call for removing the last vestiges of genocidal slavery;

although a grotesque and disorienting action in itself, the elimination of civil rights for Jews in Germany is the beginning of the escalation toward genocide (a teleological narrative that would not suit the African-American example). The call for extending democracy to everyone, based on a model of civil rights, fits with our "imagined communities of nationalism" even if this assimilative model, drawing as it does on the experience of white ethnic immigrants in the United States, fails to describe the circumstances of those brought here forcibly *to* genocidal conditions or those here before us submitted to them. That even U.S. progressives have a deep ideological and political investment in the arguments of legal personhood is clarified in *Nationalisms and Sexualities,* which notes a convergence between the "persistence of nationalism explained as a passionate 'need,'" and "the rights of sexual minorities legitimated through a discourse of civil liberties" (Parker 1992, 2). Yet, the historical reality of slavery existing legally within democracy does not fit our national ideological fictions and is therefore always already in danger of being suppressed.

To some degree, then, the model of civil rights and tolerance used by the museum, though certainly useful, glosses over very different histories and obscures the ideological interconnections of genocidal events that "happened here" and "happened there." In other words, it is problematic to assume that, because of the history of the Holocaust, Jews can function as the best guides to the larger landscape of intolerance in this country; such an assumption imparts an overarching symbolic significance to the events of the Holocaust. And yet, to the degree that this museum and this ethnicity assume the responsibilities of representing oppressions beyond their own, they make a gesture unparalleled in the United States, a fact that dismissals of this museum as a Disneyesque theme park do not acknowledge. This museum, though flawed, is at least an ambitious first step toward putting the mechanisms of oppression (and not simply diversity) into public discourse.

Holocaust Museum as Performance Site

It is the museum-goers (along with the guards) who constitute the live, performing bodies in museums. They are the focus of a variety of performance strategies deployed by museums for the sake of "the production of knowledge taken in and taken home" (Bal 1992, 560). Some of these strategies produce the passivity and fascination of "gawking"; some induce a confirming sense of "seeing" by covering over what cannot be "seen" in the very act of offering us valuable information; and some position us to struggle *to see* at the same time we are conscious of our own difficult engagement in "seeing."

If the above applies generally to museums, it has special significance for museums that represent the Holocaust. In a museum of the dead, the critical actors are gone, and it is up to us to perform acts of reinterpretation to make meaning and memory. To some degree, then, the usual museum situation (in which we look at objects) is exploited to underscore the absence to be read in the presence of objects that stand for the violent loss of which they are only the remains. To the degree that this historical, material, human loss is allowed to remain a tangible "presence," a Holocaust museum can constitute a particular metonymic situation: inanimate material objects document and mark the loss instead of simply substituting for them through representation. In this case, the enormity of the absent referent is neither contained nor scaled down through a representation that claims its presence over the terrible absence produced by genocide.

Along with the notion of a moving spectatorship, the idea of performance relates to these Holocaust museums in the sense that they are so site specific. The museum is also a performance site in the sense that its architect, designers, and management produce representations through objects and so produce a space, a subjectivity for the spectator. In terms of the notion of the museum as performance site, the individual performance strategies are not so much at issue; rather, the museum is a complicated, crowded stage that solicits a certain spectatorial gaze through skilled presentations. Everything one sees in a museum is a production by somebody. A Holocaust museum, in particular, can be a performance environment where we are asked to change from spectator/bystander to witness, where we are asked to make our specific memory into historical memory. In a Holocaust museum, when we are really solicited to change, we are asked to become performers in the event of understanding and remembering the Holocaust. If the self-depiction of the D.C. museum as "*living* memorial" is to be accurate, it is precisely because of this spectatorial performance.

In order to explore Holocaust museums as performance sites, I need to create a working model that intersects reading strategies from cultural and performance studies. Such a model requires adding performance dimensions to de Certeau's notions of "place" and "space." It also implies expanding the concept of performance beyond the prescript of the "live" in the sense of "I'm standing up and you're watching me," however important to performance that prescript continues to be. For my purposes, place means a pre-scripted performance of interpretation, and space produces sites for multiple performances of interpretation that situate/produce the spectator as historical subject.

How is the concept of de Certeauian place related to specific performance sites that produce subjects in particular ways? Place is a site that produces and manages a delimited interpretation. Performance place, then, is narrativized in advance, and we are solicited to perform the narrative that is organized for and given to us. A clear example of such a place occurs as spectators enter the tolerance section of the Beit Hashoah: We seemingly are faced with two sets of doors by which to enter—one set, outlined in bright red light, is marked "Prejudiced" and one set, outlined in green light, is marked "Unprejudiced." In actuality, the museum makes the decision for us: the "unprejudiced" doors are just a prop, unusable; everyone is herded through the "prejudiced" doors when the computer-synchronized exhibit mechanism opens them. Although linked to a single narrative, place is more than that; it is a single performance of interpretation elicited by that narrative, in this case a forced acknowledgment of our own inevitable status as prejudiced. Moreover, our bodies are implicated in the task by performing the required movement.

How is the concept of de Certeauian space related to performance in material spaces and not simply to kinds of stories identified as space? De Certeau maintains that we all live in places but should think of them as spaces. Thus the liberating countermove that allows us to understand the experience of everyday life is a move from place to space. When linked to performance, de Certeauian space must be a site for multiple performances, multiple and so not delimited by place. And if space is a site for multiple performances by spectators, it is not just a question of interpreting. Interpretation itself becomes a kind of multiple performance: performance doesn't contain the idea of space until space is connected to multiple performances—which is to say that this kind of performance is predicated on provisional subjectivity. The environment of the museum becomes performative: not only are there multiple performances of interpretation, but the museum design provides multiple scenarios for these performances—scenarios whose relationship to each other are not narrativized in advance.

Throughout the D.C. museum, architectural detail creates a performance environment for multiple, overlapping spaces of interpretation. This especially pertains to the Hall of Witness, a huge, skewed, multistoried, glass-topped courtyard at the center of the museum to which museum-goers have free access (and which contains the museum information desk, some spaces to rest, and so on). In this hall, repeating architectural detail reverberates associatively: the curved archways in this large sculpted space of brick and metal suggest a train station for deportation; windowlike structures with geometric plates of metal covering them suggest the small spaces of restricted visibility to the outside world left after the ghettos were closed up; metal-barred windows and protruding one-bulb lights suggest the outside of a concentration camp (and structures resembling guard towers surround the glass-topped courtyard ceiling); metal doors shaped like ovens (repeated in the doors to the archive downstairs) along with metal-slatted niches, whose slats open inward, suggest the crematorium itself. These associative details resonate with the literal images documenting these historical events, but provide a greater sense of surprise and discovery, however ominous, for the spectator.

Another provisional and multiple performance of subjectivity at the D.C. museum is elicited when spectators cross metal bridges enclosed in glass. These bridges, which we cross from one part of the exhibit to another, span the Hall of Witness (i.e., the large, open courtyard below). The glass walls of the bridges have writing etched into them: on one bridge a listing of the names of predominantly Jewish towns or communities destroyed during the Holocaust, on another a listing of the first names of people killed in the Holocaust, as if to underscore the impossibility of ever listing the massive number of people killed. So, unlike the Vietnam Memorial, which used the names of specific individuals for its powerful effect, this generic death list emphasizes the destruction of a culture and a cultural body. Moreover, unlike the Vietnam Memorial, the transparent glass walls allow us to view past the inscriptions to the courtyard below.

The bridges are structured to allow us to see people moving about the courtyard, but because of its height, enclosure, and inscriptions, we cannot communicate with the people below or even be seen by them except in a shadowy way. Thus, the bridges are architecturally structured to resonate with the experience of victims—distanced from, isolated from, and ignored by an everyday world of bystanders. Moreover, the bridges become even more suggestive if we notice a photograph of the Lodz Ghetto included in the Holocaust exhibit. As Berenbaum (1993) notes, "When the Lodz ghetto was established, the trolley car system could not be rerouted around the ghetto. Three bridges were built [so] Jews could walk over the bridges that divided the ghetto" (82). With "90 per cent of its starving residents working," Lodz Ghetto was akin to a slave-labor camp located in the heart of a city, its laboring Jews undeniably visible. In no way does our walk across the bridges suggest a simple-minded "you are there" reproduction. But it does put the bystander/spectator into a process of discovery and potential transformation into witness, even into a chilling resonance with ghetto inhabitants.

My assumption here, then, is that witnessing is an active process of spectatorship rather than a passive consumption of a pre-narrated spectacle. Another possible performance of interpretation at the same site might focus more on the inscriptions than the bridges. Etched on glass, these inscriptions surround spectators, almost hovering in the air. Our perception is colored by them and the absences they gesture toward, because they are in front of everything we see. Thus names of towns and people destroyed get in the way of seeing the everyday in the courtyard. This also could serve as a larger comment on the experience of the museum itself and the way what it inscribes in individual memory filters how we see the world.

In one sense, we can understand representation in general as about place, while performance is about space. But in another sense, both place and space construct the subject as a performer. If both are performances, the *place* of performance is much more rigid, more likely to be about the spectacular or the quest for the Real. It is the possibility of multiple performances by spectators that might crisscross each other, the possibility of multiple interpretations as historical subjects, that creates a different kind of performance. The critical word is multiple, whatever the particular strategies used to achieve this. But if we think of space in relation to performance, we must think of multiple performances. It is then that the performance interpretation becomes performative.

Walking through the museum can be performative in the sense of discovering it. There has to be a cognitive moment when the spectator realizes she is doing it (spectating), when the spectator realizes she is in a doing. (She can also be in a very fixed kind of doing that is unconscious precisely because it is so fixed and pre-narrativized.) One cognitive moment at the D.C. museum hinges on how its designers located some of the video monitors showing archival film footage: they are often located at floor level in such a way that spectator crowding is required even to see what is on the screen. An extreme example occurs on the middle floor, which includes the most elaborate depictions of atrocity: in a kind of raised well are located several monitors (all showing the same thing). Spectators are already clustered tightly around the well, so later spectators must crowd in aggressively to see what the monitors depict. Once there, one views videos of grotesque medical experiments forced by Nazi doctors upon concentration camp inmates. Physical agony and humiliation. And our awareness of pushing to see is foregrounded in the process. What a performance environment like this can do, then, is allow us to experience our subjectivity in unusual ways: When we crowd around the monitors, we are turning ourselves into voyeurs (and not a community of witness). Our curiosity, even our curiosity *to see* itself is thrown back at us. We are challenged, I think, to create a more self-conscious relationship to viewing materials about atrocity and take more responsibility for what we've seen.

Close by this video well, in a glass-enclosed space with benches where we hear Auschwitz survivor testimony (no visuals), the museum exploits spatial possibilities differently. Here, in order to make out the words, we must share loose-leaf notebooks containing photocopied testimony with other museum-goers. The only other thing to look at in this space are the responses of other spectators to the painful material on atrocity. The potential for physical intimacy in the design of this exhibit space creates a site for a community of witness among strangers because we are confronted with the presence of other spectators, other bodies, with whom we must cooperate.

Thus, a Holocaust museum becomes a performance space when different activities are performed simultaneously, producing different subjectivities and different goals and aims within the incoherence of that space. It is not analogous to representational theater because no one perspective can manage it. Due to its more explicit pedagogical purpose, the Beit Hashoah does create something analogous to representational theater in some parts of its Holocaust exhibit. In the first half of this exhibit, what is presented is enclosed in raised dioramas, suggesting information that can be managed by a single representational frame. Each diorama includes the same three figures—a historian, a researcher, and an exhibit designer—cast out of plaster, three-quarter sized (scale as a way of manipulating performance space), and unmoving. They could function in a self-referential way to make viewers aware of the constructedness of the narrative being presented, but they actually constitute another fixed frame for making meaning within the diorama proscenium frame. Although the three "characters" can't "perform" physically on stage, media technologies such as voice-overs represent them, and films and videos that relate Holocaust history do the performing. Moreover, each diorama exhibit is computer synchronized; each lights up and, after the timed presentation is finished, blacks out. Just like a little theater. Groups of spectators led by a volunteer walk from the now darkened site to the next one lighting up (against the darkness of the larger space for spectator movement) in the prescribed path. This mode of framed display means spectators have more equal access to the Holocaust information, since, like much theater, it is arranged to be visible and audible from as many positions as possible. But the guarantee to each viewer of an equal place comes at the price of restricted movement, passivity in response to "the show," and a place everyone engages in and moves through in a standardized way.

Holocaust History and "Manageability"

The exhibition was designed, in a number of places, to make you feel confused, disoriented, closed in. The same way that the people who lived during the Holocaust felt. It's narrow in more than one place during the exhibition. You think everything is going all right, you've come into a lot of space, and then all of a sudden it gets narrow again. It creates a mood. The whole exhibition.
—Museum guard at the U.S. Memorial Holocaust Museum,
spoken to the author

You have to personalize the story. We are using technology to that end.
—Rabbi Marvin Hier, founder and dean of the Simon Wiesenthal Center,
about the Beit Hashoah (Anderson 1993)

In answer to the problematic question of "How can we know the Holocaust?" both museums try to impart knowledge, not only about the history of these events, but about how to remember the Holocaust, how to make memory and experience performatively. Ostensibly, then, the project of both museums is to make the unmanageable history of the Holocaust manageable. This effort to make accessible to us what cannot be absorbed into anything other than itself is both highly ambitious and impossible.

Much of the U.S. Memorial Holocaust Museum presents the history of the Holocaust as an accretion of detail. The irony is that in an effort to make the unmanageable manageable through this accretion of detail (place), the D.C. museum produces a sense of unmanageability (space). The use of artifacts and dense documentation to produce knowledge and historical presence, and to shape memory, also convey the incommensurability of the loss by making this density unmanageable for the viewer. What is critical about the D.C. museum, then, in its use of small bits of everything—shoes, documents, photographs, artifacts—is the sheer, unbearable magnitude of detail. An example of the way we are made to enact this unmanageability of detail occurs at what I refer to as the tower of pictures. During the exhibit, we must cross via walkways through a tower of pictures that is taller than the exhibit's three stories. The enlarged photographs, taken between 1890 and 1941, convey the quality of Jewish life and culture that was extinguished in the Polish town of Ejszyszki, where almost no one Jewish survived. One virtue of these pictures is that they represent how these people wanted to be seen, rather than how the Nazis made them look or how they looked when the liberators found them. But while the photographs' arrangement in the structure of a tower keeps directing us to look up, the top photos are so high they recede into invisibility. So we rehearse with our bodies not only the immeasurability of the loss, but the imperfect structure of memory itself. This is one of many spaces in the museum that call for physical activity in combination with our hermeneutic and emotional activity.

Insofar as history also is an accretion of human detail, of lists, of too much, the museum offers the unmanageability of history itself. Moreover, these details represent only fragments of the people and the genocidal event that killed them. Thus the museum conveys the unmanageability of this particular genocidal history, and the unmanageability of the detail of that history. Accretion of detail, then, makes the Holocaust not just a fearful absence, but totally unmanageable in a cognitive sense. In doing so it points to the terrifying abyss, the horrific rupture, that is the history of the Holocaust. The shoes are a case in point.

The museum's choice to include a room full of nothing but piles of shoes is effective, in part because shoes are malleable enough to retain the shape of their individual owners and, even, here and there, an impractical bow or a tassel. So each shoe provides a small, intimate remnant of survival in the loss; collected in piles, the shoes convey the magnitude of that loss without becoming abstracted or aestheticized. The piles of shoes metonymically represent the huge body of shoes collected by the Nazis, which, in turn, metonymically represent the murdered people who wore them, and in so doing convey the unmanageability of the history to which they point. In their very materiality the shoes represent at once absence and presence. Moreover, despite constantly blowing fans, the shoes smell (from their own disintegration) and thus involve our bodies in making memory. The smell of the shoes is organic, like a live body, and in that way they become performers, standing in for the live bodies that are absent. Thus the shoes, as objects made to perform an absent subjectivity, are performative. Their accumulated detail buttresses the specificity of who has been lost, while we performatively enact the trajectory of memory in relation to them. To borrow Peggy Phelan's words in *Unmarked: The Politics of Performance* (1993), the shoes, as objects made to perform, do "not reproduce" what is lost, but "rather help us to restage and restate the effort to remember what is lost" (147). The performativity of the shoes "rehearses and repeats the disappearance of the subject who longs always to be remembered" (147).

In fact, the D.C. museum seems to acknowledge in its very architecture that such a modernist project of accretion is only a rearguard effort to produce manageability. The sense of this history as absence and as loss echoes through the great empty halls that alternate with the densely detailed exhibits. These large spaces of absence become part of the performance space: the horrific notion of absence, which is all one can really experience of the slaughter, is built into the museum architecture itself. Edifice produces edification. Inviting us into emptiness allows us an awareness of the unseeable of genocide. And, by creating subtle links among objects, repeating structures and movement elicited from spectators, the D.C. museum provides resonances that are not limited to one narrative performance but position spectators to perform in spaces that are, ultimately, unmanageable.

Even the seeming obviousness of the ideological envelope of democracy and liberation that encases the museum is overlapped with a subtler narrative that could render the ideological narrative unmanageable. There are repeating metal gates throughout the inside and surrounding the outside of the museum (including the loading dock). They look, at first glance, like prison doors and so seem to fit in with the resonating architectural details I mentioned earlier. But, unobtrusively located among other exhibits is the artifact that inspired this repeating design: the double gates of a Jewish cemetery, brought here, to North America. They signify the desecrated realm of the Jewish dead. But the echoes of the cemetery gates encircling the museum also suggest another enveloping structure for the museum itself: we move in the topography of the desecrated dead of Jewish genocide whenever we enter this museum. The gates of the cemetery and the gates of the museum make it clear that the whole museum is a graveyard. Notably, even the presidential inscriptions on the outside of the museum that confirm the "Americanness" of this project also look like inscriptions on giant tombstones, so that not even the most obvious ideological narrative is wholly manageable. The gates, in relation to the cemetery, lend the museum a sense of unreality; it bursts out of the boxes, the containment, of the usual museum exhibit.

While the D.C. museum acknowledges that it can never manage, the Beit Hashoah museum in L.A. primarily asserts, however reverentially, the manageability of Holocaust history and of its relation to our experience and worldview. In this it foregrounds its use of postmodern technologies, its applications of what Constance Penley and Andrew Ross (1991) term "technoculture," with its "postmodernist celebrations of the technological" and its employment of "new information and media technologies" (xii). It relies much more on computer-synchronized and computer-created exhibits, which, in a way, reduce history to information that then can be simulated and re-simulated through various performance technologies. Unlike the D.C. museum, then, which presents its spectators with an accretion of detail, the Beit Hashoah museum provides its spectators with an accretion of information, thereby suggesting that technologies in the current historical moment can re-enact the events of the Holocaust in a coherent, complete narrative of memory.

That these media technologies are performance technologies is made especially clear when, as in this museum, they are used to simulate and invoke live presence. The "Agent Provocateur," as the museum calls him in its publicity—the white male middle-class guide to the tolerance exhibit who is designed to express "polite" or unthinking intolerance—repeatedly turns up. He appears as/on a pile of video monitors, each one a screen for a different part of his body. Since he only simulates tolerance in the first place, simulating him on multiple screens (like a creature with multiple media parts threatening to impinge on our frames of reference) is an effective visual deconstruction, as well as a comment on his cultural ubiquity.

The techniques of simulation (combined with the 1960s-era exhibit technologies of the three-quarter sized plaster cast figures in the dioramas) employed to perform live presence are more problematic as used in the Holocaust section. In general at the Beit Hashoah, what is heard by visitors is privileged over what is read. Here music is used to narrativize our emotions in advance throughout the exhibit. Actor voice-overs, most often performing survivor testimony, are heard throughout as well. We are offered a kind of "you are there" melodrama of plaster figures seated at tables in a cafe (not in a diorama, but at our level) with voices of actors representing the figures' conversations about whether they should flee 1930s Germany. We are then given a narrative of what happened to each of them; it turns out these were "real" people whose situations are simulated to create a theater of identification for us.

Finally, one diorama contains a holographic image of the table at Wannsee at which the "final solution" was planned. The table is littered with glasses, filled ashtrays, and so on (while voice-overs convey the Nazi presence). I know this "scene" ought to induce horror, but when I saw it, I was fascinated by the simulation itself and how it was made, as well as faintly embarrassed that I was peering at it as I would into a department-store window. What I'm suggesting is that, because of what it seeks to depict, in this part of the museum, simulation as a performance technology actually incorporates fairly traditional modes of representation in its simulations of live presence. Moreover, because in simulation there is no link to the referent anymore, the copy passes itself off as the real, thereby covering over the historical trauma of the incommensurable absence of the genocidal referent. More successful is another section of the museum, called "The Other America." It includes a large wooden colored map of the United States that charts the locations, state by state, of 250 hate groups. By touching a computer screen, visitors can choose to learn more about each group, but the entire body of information would be unmanageable for a viewer. The map, itself frighteningly effective, is made more so by the use of computers, thereby combining low and high tech to create an unmanageable space.

In general, the Beit Hashoah stages a postmodern project of presenting history as a flow of information. Sometimes it is a "one-way flow" of information (places for single performances of interpretation); sometimes there is a "multidirectional distribution of cultural and data flows" (spaces for multiple performances of interpretation) (Penley and Ross 1991, x-xi). Interestingly, one of the most extensive sites for multiple performances at the Beit Hashoah occurs in hyperspace. When visitors come in, they are directed to the top floor of the museum first. This floor contains an archival collection room; the rest of the floor is devoted to computer stations. Volunteer greeters of various ages and genders welcome us to these computers, urging us to play with them, and giving us any information we might need to operate them. We need very little. At the D.C. museum, the computers seem only to point users to well-presented films of survivor testimony or to sounds of Jewish music; however, any other information is hard to access. This creates a de Certeauian place in hyperspace. But at the Beit Hashoah, we need only touch the screen with one finger and more information is provided. Everything seems connected to everything else, so each visitor can create multiple paths for information and multiple relationships among the Holocaust information offered.

If the D.C. museum alternates between intensity of detail and spaces of absence, neither of which is manageable, the Beit Hashoah creates manageability through simulation and a scaled-down narrative of Holocaust history. Moreover, in its focus on tolerance, the Beit Hashoah simulates social problems and prejudices in a way that asserts their manageability (i.e., places masquerading as interactive spaces) even if they exist on sixteen different television screens at the same time. In a structure like a video arcade, multiple "tolerance" games can be played in any order. It is frenetic and noisy there. But the games are all abstracted encounters with difference that ultimately lead to the same one narrative about tolerance. In general, however, the way the L.A museum's presentations are configured under the rubric of information makes them more available for contemporary linkages among differing cultural concepts and historical events related to the theme of intolerance. Nonetheless, because of its urgent desire for narrative connections to the present, it is less available than the D.C. museum for the project of making memory and witness in response to the historical events of the Holocaust, except in a space of absence called the Hall of Testimony. This hall is at the end of the Holocaust section, and made of concrete, with concrete benches and raised video monitors encased in concrete. It is a big, cold, window-less room, suggestive of a bunker or a crematorium. Holocaust survivor testimony and the words of those who did not survive play on the monitors. Between showings of individual narratives, cantorial voices sing. The voices are full of sorrow that cannot be managed, full of the weight of a history that cannot be absorbed, absences that can never be filled, contradictions that can never be resolved.

Notes

1. For example, on April 19, 1993, three days before the U.S. Holocaust Memorial Museum actually opened, front-page news for the Bowling Green *Sentinel-Tribune* (and I'm sure many other local newspapers) included an article entitled "Survey: One in 5 Doubt Holocaust Happened." A Holocaust survey (referred to as "the first systematic study of Americans' knowledge of the Nazi's extermination of six million Jews before and during World War II") done by the Roper Organization in the United States in November of 1992 and provided by the American Jewish Committee, sampled 992 adults. To the question "Does it seem possible or does it seem impossible to you that the Nazi extermination of the Jews never happened?" 22 percent said, "It seems possible" it never happened, 65 percent said, "It seems impossible" it never happened, and 12 percent replied with, "Don't know/No answer." These statistics were framed in a box next to the article.

Furthermore, the Roper Survey found "that thirty-eight percent of adults and fifty-three percent of high school students did not know the meaning of the term the Holocaust." The information presented here, as well as its placement in time, constitutes a kind of self-evident rationale for an American Holocaust museum (though the museum is never directly mentioned) or for a Holocaust pedagogy in U.S. public schools, potentially increasing a favorable reception among the four out of five who believe it is impossible that the Nazi extermination never happened.

2. As Jim Young notes in *The Texture of Memory* (1993), "Over time, the only 'common' experience uniting an otherwise diverse, often fractious, community of Jewish Americans has been the vicarious memory of the Holocaust. Left-wing and right-wing Jewish groups, religious and secular, Zionist and non-Zionist may all draw different conclusions from the Holocaust. But all agree that it must be remembered, if to entirely disparate ideological ends" (348).

3. On the April 18, 1993, Op-Ed page of the *New York Times,* Jonathan Rosen, editor of *The Forward,* quotes Michael Berenbaum, who was the direc-

tor of the projected museum, as saying, "What we are about is the Americaniza-
tion of the Holocaust." In response, Rosen critiqued the soon-to-open museum
as "building a shrine to Jewish victimization" and so inscribing this (Christian-
created) role of suffering onto Jews within an American context. What interests
me is the underlying debate this exchange represents: Will publicizing and creating a pedagogy for conveying the historical sufferings and injustices imposed
upon a particular group result in better treatment for that group in the present?
Or will it reinscribe their position as sufferers, possibly rationalizing or setting a
precedent for further suffering? Neither assumption per se suggests fitting the
historical events of the Holocaust into a discourse emphasizing the larger structures that produce atrocity and oppression, although Holocaust educational
groups like the Facing History Project do try to include this in their pedagogy.
Nor does either of the two link this "Americanized" Jewish narrative of suffering and oppression to the production of other discourses of historical suffering
and oppression currently circulating: "founding" narratives crucial (however
"essentialized") to the struggle against injustice, especially when configured
under the rubric of identity politics. It is at the Beit Hashoah Museum of Tolerance, in L.A., that museum designers have tried to place, however imperfectly,
this history of Jewish suffering in relation to that of other groups, most notably
African Americans.

4. Actually, the Washington Monument, by means of which the museum
locates itself within a national landscape, was also privately sponsored on government land. For an analysis of the political and funding history of the Washington Monument, see Savage 1992.

5. Over the years the museum has increased its efforts to depict the histories
of Gypsies, homosexuals, Jehovah's Witnesses, and the handicapped. For example, the spring 1997 special issue of *Update: United States Holocaust Memorial
Museum* contains the article "Gay and Lesbian Campaign Passes $1 Million
Mark." These funds are to go to two activities: "an endowment for the study of
homosexuals in the Holocaust" and "the further documentation of gay oral histories, location of artifacts for the permanent collection, lectures and special programs" (*Update,* supplement 2). The museum also coordinated an exhibit of
artifacts related to the "experiences of homosexuals living under Nazism" during
the time the NAMES Project Memorial Quilt was on display in Washington.

6. More interesting in terms of the use of computers in relation to the
Holocaust is the display, within the exhibit, of the Hollerith, a very early data-
processing device. This device enabled the Nazis to assert in 1934, "We are
recording the individual characteristics of every single member of the nation
onto a little card," thus using technology as a means to impose and process the
essentialized "characteristics" used to constitute people into groups. While these
data were used to persecute Jews and other groups, the reference to "every
single member of the nation" recollects the way in which persecution is interre-

lated with the regulation and containment of the population as a whole. Such reduction of the population to life-affirming or life-denying data ought to clarify the stakes for "normative" groups in resisting genocidal actions.

7. The Global Documentation Room is made to resemble a newsroom in order to give viewers a sense of both immediacy and objectivity. However, as Barbara Harlow (1996) states, human rights reporting is both a genre and a mode of intervention, and not only documentation:

Human rights reporting, itself a genre in the contemporary world of writing and rights, entails both documentation and intervention. A recording of facts and events, of abuses of individual lives and national histories, as well as an effort to correct an official record that has systematically obscured those abuses, the writing of human rights draws of necessity on conventions of narrative and auto/biography, of dramatic representation, and of discursive practice. (38)

Some of the museum's educational events and talks are about a wide variety of both internally and internationally persecuted groups; these represent an attempt to take its mission beyond documentation.

8. For example, in 1992, *Connection Journal,* a newsletter for gay Seventh-Day Adventists, reproduced a letter it clearly does not support by a group called The Oregon Citizens Alliance, which call for "God's solutions," namely the "Execution, Castration, and Imprisonment" of homosexuals (1). In a distinct echo of Nazism (or is it McCarthyism?), the Alliance solicits "the names of suspected or self admitted homosexuals" for its "Homosexual Names-Collection Division" (1). Having buttressed my argument with this horrific example, it's worth noting in general that ejaculations of hate from the far right may exert their own spectacular lure for us as a way of quickly validating whatever operates against it.

9. For such an exploration and reconfiguring of American democracy, see Brian Wallis's *Democracy: A Project by Group Material* (1990) and Chantal Mouffe's "Radical Democracy: Modern or Postmodern?" (1988).

Works Cited

Bal, Mieke. 1992. "Telling, Showing, Showing Off." *Critical Inquiry* 18 (spring): 556-94.

Berenbaum, Michael. 1990. "The Uniqueness and Universality of the Holocaust." *A Mosaic of Victims: Non-Jews Persecuted and Murdered by the Nazis.* Ed. Berenbaum. New York: New York UP.

———. 1993. *The World Must Know: The History of the Holocaust as Told in the United States Holocaust Memorial Museum.* Boston: Little.

Bourne, Jenny. 1987. "Homelands of the Mind: Jewish Feminism and Identity Politics." *Race and Class: A Journal for Black and Third World Liberation* 29.1 (summer): 1-24.

Certeau, Michel de. 1984. *The Practice of Everyday Life.* Trans. Steven Rendall. Berkeley: U of California P.

Gourevitch, Philip. 1993. "Behold Now Behemoth: The Holocaust Memorial Museum: One More American Theme Park." *Harper's* 287.1718 (July): 55-62.

Harlow, Barbara. 1996. "From the 'Civilizing Mission' to 'Humanitarian Interventionism': Postmodernism, Writing, and Human Rights." *Text and Nation.* Ed. Peter C. Pfeiffer and Laura Garcia-Moreno. Columbia, SC: Camden. 31-47.

Lipstadt, Deborah. 1993. *Denying the Holocaust: The Growing Assault on Truth and Memory.* New York: Free.

Mouffe, Chantal. 1988. "Radical Democracy: Modern or Postmodern?" Trans. Paul Holdengraber. *Universal Abandon? The Politics of Postmodernism.* Ed. Andrew Ross. Minneapolis: U of Minnesota P. 31-45.

"Oregon Citizens Alliance." 1992. *Connection Journal: A Community Newsletter for Seventh-day Adventist Kinship International* 16.8 (Oct.).

Parker, Andrew, et al., eds. 1992. *Nationalisms and Sexualities.* New York: Routledge.

Penley, Constance, and Andrew Ross, eds. 1991. *Technoculture.* Cultural Politics 3. Minneapolis: U of Minnesota P.

Phelan, Peggy. 1993. *Unmarked: The Politics of Performance.* New York: Routledge.

Rosen, Jonathan. 1993. "The Misguided Holocaust Museum." *New York Times* April 18: Op-Ed section.

Savage, Kirk. 1992. "The Self-made Monument: George Washington and the Fight to Erect a National Memorial." *Critical Issues in Public Art: Content, Context, and Controversy.* Ed. Harriet F. Senie and Sally Webster. New York: Harper. 5-32.

Wallis, Brian, ed. 1990. *Democracy: A Project by Group Material.* Discussions in Contemporary Culture 5, sponsored by the DIA Art Foundation. Seattle: Bay.

Wyman, David S. 1984. *The Abandonment of the Jews: America and the Holocaust 1941-1945.* New York: Pantheon.

Young, James E. 1992. "America's Holocaust: Memory and the Politics of Identity." Paper presented for "The Holocaust and the American Jewish Imagination: Memory, Text, and Myth" panel. Modern Language Association Conference. December.

——. 1993. *The Texture of Memory: Holocaust Memorials and Meaning.* New Haven: Yale UP.

Epilogue

THE INDIVIDUAL AND COLLECTIVE SEARCH FOR IDENTITY

Dena Elisabeth Eber and Arthur G. Neal

The search for identity in modern society stems from a sense of incompleteness. As a people, we do not know who we are collectively or where we are headed as we move into the future. History has not yet completed its exploration of the limits of human nature or its experimentation on the many possible relationships between the individual and society. We have no conception of society as mature or fully developed. There is no overriding notion comparable to the idea from ancient China that the boundaries of the Empire constitute the boundaries of the moral universe. Instead, our historical epoch is characterized by a future orientation and an emphasis on society as continuously being in a state of growth and development. Because our collective identity is constantly shifting, our appetite to find out who we are individually seems to be insatiable.

Cultural traditions as blueprints for behavior have weakened with industrial and technological development, and new forms of freedom have emerged. If we knew who we were collectively and if we had a more clearly defined historical guide to the future, the study of memory and representation would be less necessary than it now is. We no longer have a society in which the place of the individual in the broader scheme of social affairs is clear and definite. The stability of social ties that characterized our historical past has been broken, and increases in freedom of movement have uprooted us. The result is a historical increase in psychological dependence on personal resources in times of trouble. Coping with the changing conditions of our society, responding to the changes occurring within ourselves, and elaborating on the meaning of social events are among the many aspects of modern awareness.

An identity crisis is especially acute for those who view the overall drift of modern society as chaotic, unpredictable, and bereft of purpose. Such views of society make it difficult for the individual to engage in long-range planning with a reasonable degree of confidence. Instead individuals often respond by developing a limited time perspective, by emphasizing the here and now, and by accepting the hedonistic view that one should live for today and let tomorrow take care of itself. To a significant degree, faith in long-term planning of one's life is dependent upon being able to see how events are interrelated and predictable.

This generation is making a sharp separation between self and society, but it is a separation that cannot be sustained adequately on purely theoretical grounds. The individual is both a producer and a product of social life in its varied forms. The performances that give shape to behavior are in part socially imposed and in part self-generated. Individuals who act out of an awareness of others necessarily take each other into account and have their behaviors shaped and modified in the process. Humans are indeed adaptable creatures, and the cumulative effects of the decisions made by millions of people shape their identities and their futures. The effects are then passed on to future generations that frequently lack awareness of the sources of their personal knowledge.

People extract additional meanings from the world around them in order to enhance basic values and objectives. Just as we have turned our attention outward to the exploration of space, we are also turning our attention inward to examine the subjective qualities of life. Within this context we may reasonably expect a great deal of interest in experimenting with new forms of social organization and social living. To the extent that this is so, humans appear to have the capacity to shape their own destinies within certain limits; and these limits may be very broad indeed. Human awareness and intentions enter into the matrix of social causation, along with many other factors in shaping the course of social events.

We agree with Daniel C. Dennett's observation (1996, 57) that "[the] mind is fundamentally an anticipator, an expectation-generator. It mines the present for clues, which it refines with the help of materials it has saved from the past, turning them into anticipations of the future." The collision between new experiences and old memories frequently results in competition for domination and control of behavior. From the complexity of modern life, the individual is often unable to meet his or her minimal standards for clarity in decision-making and action. Conflicts grow out of the multiple realities individuals encounter in the social realm, and competing truth claims reduce the capacity of individuals to see how personal and social events are connected. In effect, decisive lines of action are stymied by personal knowledge that is incoherent, skewed, and not at all free from contradictions.

The sense that something is missing in personal lives stems in part from the accelerated rate of technological change in recent years. The spread of sophisticated technology and the growth of economic interdependency convey numerous implications for the conditions under which men and women live. What once was purely local subsequently became national and what was exclusively national has now become global. The speed, efficiency, and availability of modern transportation, combined with the rising standards of living during the twentieth century, produced an acceleration of exposure to cultures other than one's own. This has reduced the importance of local events in shaping personal identities.

The Global and the Local

Through communications technology, private spaces were opened up to the outside world, and correspondingly the outer world increasingly penetrated personal space. Such developments grew out of a willingness to escape from the privacy of personal lives into wider communities. As a result, global influences now exist as the horizon within which we frame our personal existence. For example, in the past we thought of the home as a private place, a place to retreat from the world, a place that was "off limits" without a specific invitation to enter. Today the typical living room has become a place where global events impinge upon local space (Meyrowitz 1985). Being connected to the total world is reflected in the presence of a mailbox, a telephone, a radio, a television set, a VCR, and a computer linked to the Internet and the World Wide Web. People's identities are built around immediate experiences, and these immediate experiences are becoming global in character.

If globalization trends continue, national boundaries will mean less and less, and cultural differences will increasingly become muted as more and more people begin to have enough in common to share a transnational identity. With increased global connectivity, the people of the world will increasingly share forms of symbolic representation that were once limited to local cultures and communities (Tomlinson 1999). These include sharing narratives on how life may be lived, pictures of ideal human relations, versions of human fulfillment, sources of personal meaning, and what people draw upon to make sense out of their existence. It is through such accounts that globalization promotes the rapid spread of new cultural forms.

The quest for a deeper awareness of the universal has prompted an accelerated emphasis upon international travel for recreation and leisure. Fewer and fewer people are living out their lives within the confines of the nation in which they were born. International travel involves a quest for authentic experiences that cannot be obtained from just reading a book or watching a television documentary. It also reflects an interest in transcending the mundane aspects of everyday life by seeking a firmer linkage with a broader framework of the human condition. By "being there" the tourist has direct and personal experiences that stand in contrast to the vicarious and indirect experiences of the television viewer.

Mass entertainment and international travel have resulted in the exposure of a large number of individuals to cultures and lifestyles that extend far beyond their immediate and limited spheres of direct experience. As a result, cosmopolitan worldviews are replacing worldviews that in earlier times were primarily local in character (Giddens 1990). The cosmopolitan worldview involves an awareness of global connectivity as having significance for one's personal well-being; placing a value on personal mobility and foreign travel; and being open to cultural influences and appreciating cultural differences.

Cosmopolitanism also involves an awareness of a world that is comprised of many cultures, a willingness to question the assumptions of one's own traditions; and a recognition of cultural relativity and pluralism so long as human rights are not being violated. The research of Rebecca Green (chapter 1) is an excellent example of a specific cultural elaboration that taps into universal aspects of the human experience. Humans are aware of their mortality, and this awareness sets them apart from all other animals. But when death occurs, it necessarily constitutes a trauma for those who are close friends or family members of the deceased. The ritualistic re-wrapping of the dead in Madagascar reflects an attempt to hold on to the deceased person, to maintain an ongoing relationship with the dead, and to establish both a practical and an emotional linkage between the past, the present, and the future. Further, this cultural performance surrounding death gives the descendants an identity, for without this physical memory of their ancestors, they lack a self. An important reference point is provided for placing human tragedy within a framework of meaning, commitment, and self-actualization.

In all cultures, the corpse is viewed as an extraordinary entity to be treated with reverence and respect. While the corpse is generally viewed as a sacred object, there are conditions that require viewing it from a secular, mundane standpoint. This secular view is evident in Kathleen Dixon's research (chapter 2) on the use of cadavers to train students in medical school. Yet, while dissecting a cadaver is an essential part of medical education, students are seldom free from the ambivalence that grows out of the secular treatment of what is generally viewed as a sacred object in our society. In fact, many were shocked at how they not only identified with the cadaver, but saw themselves, a mortal of flesh and bones, mirrored in the corpse. They were often stunned because they believed they were distant from the flesh they were dissecting, that is, until they encountered it. Perhaps the cadaver represented flesh memory of their humanness, a reminder of who they are and what will come of them. If American medical students held the reverence for the dead that is found in Madagascar, they would be incapacitated in their gross anatomy classes.

Systems of culture reflect human hopes and aspirations as well as the deepest fears and anxieties. While social norms are created to keep social relationships orderly and predictable, all societies must deal with evil and abnormality in some manner or another. The study by Kathryn Farr (chapter 3) of the women on death row documents the process by which certain individuals are designated as evil and treated accordingly. Through the several forms of representing evil, the members of a society are provided with guidelines on the rules for defining socially unacceptable conduct and the moral boundaries that are not to be crossed within any given social system. This system, although local, has global implications for definitions of evil and hence, the designation of specific individuals as immoral persons.

Traumatic Memories

The selective and arbitrary character of memory in everyday life stands in contrast to the imprinting that occurs under conditions of crisis and trauma. Because our memories shape who we are, traumatic events play a profound role in shaping the self. The lingering consequences of trauma require that we conceptually modify our usual way of looking at memory and representation. Under normal circumstances, past experiences provide us with a storehouse of information that may be drawn upon when it is useful to do so. However, when memories of the war veteran, the rape victim, or the sexually abused child (see Beerman and Haraszti, chapter 6) become traumatic, they are no longer useful. Instead, they are uncontrollable, a source of discomfort, and unwanted.

The emotions tapped by trauma grow out of what it means to be human. Universally, the elements of trauma include some level of shock, disbelief, and pain. Everyday assumptions about the world as friendly, meaningful, and just are shattered (Janoff-Bulman 1992). Because of the suffering associated with trauma, individuals are unable to remain emotionally detached or indifferent. Heightened emotionality is expressed in intense forms of sadness, anger, and fear. The cognitive processing of information is superseded by the terror that accompanies intense feelings of helplessness.

Under conditions of intense fear, several things happen physiologically. Fear leads to heightened production of adrenaline, to an increase in the sugar level in the bloodstream and to other stress responses that mobilize an organism for "fight or flight." The physiological reactions alter the central nervous system and result in deep imprinting of memory traces (Herman 1992). These memory traces, or memory fragments, have a tenacious quality about them and recur on a sporadic basis.

Trauma nightmares and intrusive memories are geared toward achieving closure to the event. Such efforts reflect what is called "the Zigarnik effect" in psychology. This principle refers to the importance of "the completion tendency" in human affairs. We tend to remember more vividly unfinished tasks than the ones that have been completed. For example, unwanted memories of trauma continue to surface until some degree of closure is achieved. The more intense traumatic memories tend to be nonverbal, static, and repetitious. They more nearly appear as a series of still snapshots or like a silent movie, rather than as a coherent narrative (Herman 1992).

In many ways it would be preferable for the rape victim or the war veteran simply to forget the past and pretend that the traumatic event did not occur. However, this is not a reasonable possibility. Reenactments of the trauma will appear in unintended and uncontrollable ways. These not only include the intrusive memories that surface during the waking hours, but also such sleep disorders as insomnia, startle awakenings, and terrifying nightmares. Other maladaptive responses include eating disorders, feelings of estrangement from others, impaired memory, difficulty in concentrating on everyday tasks, a sense of emptiness, and psychological numbing.

Recovery for the trauma victim requires confronting the event in question and placing it within the framework of viable assumptions about the nature of social life and the qualities and attributes of other people. Fragments of traumatic events continue to surface until some degree of closure is achieved (Janoff-Bulman 1992). Unwanted memories tend to dissipate in intensity only after completing the process of linking traumatic experiences to everyday assumptions about social life as friendly, meaningful, and predictable.

Direct encounters with extraordinary forms of evil cannot be understood in terms of either previous social learning or beliefs about living in a just world. The long-term effects of massive psychic trauma have been evident in research on survivors of the Nazi Holocaust. The enormity of the suffering endured by survivors includes coping with the stigma that accompanies victimization, living with generalized attitudes of suspicion and distrust, and having a sense of psychological isolation (Kahana et al. 1997). The sense of estrangement from others derives from having had intense personal experiences that cannot be shared with others. Talking about the "unspeakable" engenders a sense of discomfort for either the speaker or the listener or both. From a combination of silence and stigma, Holocaust survivors were thrown back on their own resources. The usual social support network failed to operate at the times they were needed. To cope with the experience, be it a survivor or someone who endured the war, many initially denied the atrocities they witnessed or felt. However, some eventually confronted their memories through other means such as art. For example, Josepha Haveman's WarTime !: is a digitally based animation that represents some of her childhood memories associated with the holocaust. The work incorporates sound, illustration, and photographs to relive and face some of the memories she buried about her experience with the war. You may view excerpts and text from her animation on-line at: http://www. imagecircle.com/WarTime.html

Giving official recognition to an ugly past is a very difficult task. It brings to the surface painful memories and conveys implications for the human prospect that are disturbing (Maier 1988; Kramer 1996). This has been evident in the debates in the academic community both in Germany and elsewhere over the implications of the Nazi Holocaust for German national identity (Lowenthal 1996). Debates over the Holocaust frequently center around whether this event was unique among the atrocities in human history or whether it was simply a type of event that has occurred at many times and places.

Those who relativize the Holocaust tend to downplay its lasting significance for German national identity. Some argue that it was "the Nazis," rather than the German people, who committed those unspeakable atrocities. In contrast, those who see the type and scope of the atrocities as unsurpassed in human history maintain that Germany must confront in some major way the significance of this event for a national identity. In similar fashion, the politics of memory is reflected in debates over what form of commemoration, atonement, or remembrance would be appropriate for such a difficult past.

The creation of Holocaust museums is based on the assumption that it is important for subsequent generations to remember what some regard as the ultimate representation of terror and evil (see Patraka, chapter 8). Yet the problem of creating a usable past becomes an extremely difficult one. Attempts to portray the Nazi Holocaust in the creative arts run the risk of either re-victimizing the survivors or trivializing the horrors they experienced. However, the duty to remember stands in contrast to the desire to forget. As collective traumas become embedded in the social heritage of any given group of people, the desire to deny what happened stands in sharp contrast with the perceived necessity to speak loudly about the terrible events that occurred, thus creating many interpretations of the truth or reality.

Multiple Realities

As we go about our daily activities, we are aware of the reality of our own existence, the reality of other people, and the reality of the objects and events that enter into our consciousness. These realities as we know them are constructed from our own experiences and organized into systems of meaning. We tend to act with some level of confidence about the adequacy of our understanding of the event in which we are engaged. We hold some level of probability for successful mastery and control over the outcomes we seek, and we assign some degree of reward value to the relationships we have established with others.

Because our experiences, imaginations, and life circumstances differ, we do not share the same realities but live in a world with a diversity of meaning. Our own understanding of events is not fully congruent with the perceptions of others. For example, the realities of the classroom are not the same for the professor as for the students. The professor has control over the available learning resources, already knows what the students are expected to learn, and speaks with authority in delivering lectures and in directing class discussions. The aims and objectives of the students and the professor may be similar in several respects, but the perspectives brought to bear on the situation are likely to vary. The students themselves are varied in the intensity with which they listen; they hear different things; and they give different interpretations to what the professor and other students say.

American society is not the same for the dominant, white majority as it is for racial and ethnic minority groups; the system is not the same for men as it is for women; nor the same for the super-rich as for those caught up in poverty. While those in privileged positions are inclined to see the world as a friendly place where justice prevails, those who are socially disadvantaged are likely to view the world as unfriendly and unreceptive to personal needs and interests.

In the twenty-first century, as in the recent past, identities will be layered along a continuum from local to global. In the early years of life, gender and the family of origin constitute the core of a self-identity. As individuals move through the life course, additional identities are added and layered. These include, for example, educational level, occupational status, religious affiliation, marital status, community of residence, political party affiliation, ethnicity, and the national state.

Increased cultural complexity results in a greater variety of answers to the question of "who am I?" Instead of a single, overriding answer to this question, multiple answers are given to the identity question. As a result, loyalties and commitments, for most people, are spread across a variety of social groups. From multiple and overlapping group memberships, there is no one particular group that can make a legitimate claim of total access to the individual's time and effort. Since loyalties and allegiances are spread across several identities, individuals are provided with a greater freedom of movement than existed in previous societies.

Variations in lifestyles occur over time as a result of different degrees of exposure to changing historical circumstances. Young people presumably have greater receptivity to changing norms, values, and attitudes than do older people that continue with lifestyles shaped during an earlier period of time. We may note, for example, the different circumstances of growing up during the conditions of scarcity and hardship of the Great Depression of the 1930s as compared to growing up during the times of prosperity and material well-being of the 1950s and 1960s. Those growing up during the Great Depression had direct experiences with high rates of unemployment and economic hardship. Through knowing what scarcities were like, they became oriented toward savings and investments (Elder 1974). In contrast, the generation entering early adulthood during the 1950s and 1960s had direct experience with economic abundance and tended to take access to the good life for granted (Simon and Gagnon 1976). They were inclined to see the older generation as overly materialistic and money oriented.

Patriotism and national pride were prominent among young people during World War II, and this stands in contrast to the hostile attitudes toward war and militarism that developed among young people during the Vietnam War. Following the Japanese attack on Pearl Harbor, the nation had been transformed into a moral community and consensus had developed on the need for promoting the war effort. In contrast, the nation was highly divided during the Vietnam War, and the youth of the nation became cynical about nationalistic and patriotic values. Thus, the orientations toward numerous aspects of social life are likely to vary according to historical circumstances and reflect different viewpoints according to age and generation level.

The divisions along generational lines have been intensified in modern society because of the extensions of the life span and greater variation in age levels. For example, during the course of the twentieth century the life expectancy increased by more than twenty-five years. Dramatic changes have sharpened the contrasts in generational experiences and intensified the fragmentation in the social realm. Historical events cannot have the same meaning for those who only hear about them as compared to those who experienced them directly.

Generations are now foremost among the divisions within the social system and thus a primary source for the pluralization of life-worlds.

Generations differ in immediate preoccupations, hold different world-views, and frequently go their separate ways. Schisms develop over difference in lifestyles and communication problems surface as each finds it difficult to accept the other's point of view.

The intersections of personal biography with historical events are crucial for many aspects of knowing who we are and what we are to become. The questions of "how did we get to where we are now," "where are we now," and "where are we headed as we move into the future" are basic to personal and collective identities. The task of the individual is to find his or her place within the broader scheme of human affairs. A primary task of a nation is that of reworking data from the past, processing many levels of truth and reality, in order to shape a contemporary identity.

The task of shaping a collective identity is embedded in the work of mass entertainment, in news journalism, in the educational system, in the creative arts, and in the work of all those specialists who are exploring the limitations and prospects of the world in which we live. These people present, or *re-present,* memories depicting many levels of truth that spar and compete with our perceptions of reality, and thus our aggregate selves.

Art, New Technology, and the Construction of Self

At no other time in history have artists had the opportunity so profoundly to challenge reality as they do now; the surge of new technology has and continues to encourage the questioning and further construction of individual identity. Although also affected globally through collective memory, artists make and remake themselves locally with every true work they create. Art has many truths, but among them and perhaps the most pervasive is the truth of artistic self-expression. In other words, a true work of art is any piece in which the artist has put an authentic part of him or herself into, a work that is in some way expressive.

Artists have always used technology, from early pigments to printing presses. However, the *new technologies* we refer to are the tools and metaphorical constructs induced from Norbert Wiener's idea of *cybernetics* (1948), the term in information-processing theory that refers to the organization of signals, both receiving and transmitting, from humans, animals, and machines, into a complex integrated system (Stiles 1996). This notion was the seed for ideas such as *cyberspace* and *cyborgs.* William Gibson coined the term cyberspace in his novel *Neuromancer* (1984), which referred to an illusionary silicon-based world that existed when the narrator "jacked into" the computer and shared data with other such silicon "cowboys." Today, we use the term cyberspace to refer to any reality we construct via digital computing, including interacting with others over networks or the Internet, or the world we create when we experience a digital video game.

Some take the notion of cyberspace to a level of lived reality, one they construct and exist in. Perhaps these spaces are inhabited by cyborgs, beings who have some of their embodied organic functions controlled by cybernetic devices (Haraway 1985). Musing on what such a being would eat, Margaret Morse (1994) used the organic need for food as a springboard to point out some problems with the cyborg life, be it fantasy, metaphor, or a perceived reality. Despite these uncertainties, there are those who either perceive their existence as part cyborg or see a future in which humans will be cyborgs. Hans Moravec (see Eber, chapter 5) envisions a time when robots will upload human consciousness to a computer and there will no longer be a need for the physical organic body.

As peculiar as some of this may sound, notions like cyborg and cyberspace have influenced the technology-driven way in which we live. Most recently, a man who called himself *dotcomguy* vowed to stay in his house for the entire year of 2000. He will acquire everything he needs, including food and human contact, via the World Wide Web. His existence and identity is silicon- and cyber-based. At the time of this writing, a user can view *dotcomguy* live by visiting his site at *www.dotcomguy. com*. The goal of his project is to show the viability of *e-commerce,* or electronic commerce, via the World Wide Web. He hopes to show that we can indeed shop, work, and have intimate relationships, all in the comfort of our own home and within the context of cyberspace. *Dotcomguy* is reinventing himself as the man who survives via the Internet. The sixteen cameras in his home reveal some slices of his reality, from which he will construct an identity.

To a small degree, we all remake ourselves when we partake in the new cyber technologies, maybe not to the extent that *dotcomguy* does, but we take on an identity based on a constructed truth of ourselves which becomes our cyber reality, or perhaps, our cyborg alter ego. Even those who do not see themselves as cyber addicts work and interact with machines much like our culture used to interact with other people. According to the personality psychologist and sociologist Sherry Turkle (1995), many people spend the bulk of their day in front of a computer or television screen. Her research on identity by way of the Internet suggests that when we "step through the screen into virtual communities, we reconstruct our identities on the other side of the looking glass. This reconstruction is our cultural work in progress" (177). In other words, we construct a reality of ourselves using new technologies. Turkle further suggests that although most of us see our bodies as real and separate from the computer, we still interact with games and programs as if the computer or the game had some kind of real existence or life to it which might include our bodies.

Considering this same influence on artists, those in our society who will most likely mirror changes, technology has strongly influenced the kind of works they produce and the truths they construct, especially the artists who use the digital medium. From profound performances of cyborg existence to more subtle manipulations of truth and reality, new technology artists are constructing a truth through their art that reflects how they, and most likely others, see themselves.

The performance artist Stelarc is an extreme example of an artist who uses technological ideas to erase the memory of his carbon-based humanness and reconstruct himself as a silicon being. His 1986 *Amplified Body, Laser Eyes, and Virtual Arm* design (Stiles 1996) was research into how he could extend his organic self into a technological being, speculating that the human form would eventually be a "human-machine symbiosis" (429). His design details the amplification of vital body sounds as a way to expose the inward body externally. It also includes a scheme for a third hand that will extend human abilities via technology. He further speculates that skin is now obsolete and "inadequate in interfacing with reality; technology has become the body's new membrane of existence" (430). Stelarc is an artist who sees the human organic form as coming to a useless end. He is thus reconstructing himself as a kind of cyborg: a reality that he performs and lives, and one that has become his constructed identity.

More subtle manifestations of artistic identity through constructed reality by means of new technology are prevalent among digital artists, especially those who create photographic-like imagery or realistic-looking animations. Artists like Martina Lopez construct digital images that embody realities from the past, representations of her family history and their lives. Her works, such as *Heirs Come to Pass 4* (1991), display people in such a way that it reads as a narrative of her ancestors. In them, her landscapes are constructed and "the horizon suggests endless time, the trees demarcate space, and the fragments of snapshots verify an actual lived experience" (Lopez 1994, 13). Here, she constructed herself through her history by fabricating a space in which she represented her family's past. She then extended this idea beyond her personal family to include the family history of others. In this way, she "creat[ed] a collective history, one that would allow people to bring their own memories to [her] work" (13). In a sense, Lopez used her art and new technology to construct imagery and a kind of truth that in effect represented her own, as well as a collective identity.

Through new technologies, artists now have more control over the realistic representation of their ideas. Coupled with the effect of new technology on our society as a whole, artists are finding new ways of shaping their memories and their resulting selves. True art is the expression of the artist's self through his or her medium, in which he or she constructs a reality that is negotiated by multiple truths.

There is an artist in each of us, and we construct our narratives though living our everyday lives. These stories are living performances of our reality, ones that become our truth, our memories, and our identity. Our narratives develop and grow as a function of our interaction with our global world. In a climate where human interaction necessarily includes new technologies, our collective identities cannot help but morph into a self which is mediated by the onslaught of silicon.

Works Cited

Dennett, Daniel C. 1996. *Kinds of Minds.* New York: Basic.

Elder, Glen H., Jr. 1974. *Children of the Great Depression.* Chicago: U of Chicago P.

Gibson, William. 1984. *Neuromancer.* New York: Ace.

Giddens, Anthony. 1990. *The Consequences of Modernity.* Cambridge: Polity.

Haraway, Donna. 1985. "A Manifesto for Cyborgs: Science, Technology, and Socialist-Femininism in the 1980s." *Socialist Review* 80: 65-108.

Herman, Judith Lewis. 1992. *Trauma and Recovery.* New York: Basic.

Janoff-Bulman, Ronnie. 1992. *Shattered Assumptions: Towards a New Psychology of Trauma.* New York: Free.

Kahana, B., E. Kahana, Z. Harel, and K. Kelly. 1997. "A Framework for Understanding the Chronic Stress of Holocaust Survivors." *Coping with Chronic Stress.* Ed. B. J. Gottlieb. New York: Plenum. 55-79.

Kramer, Jane. 1996. *The Politics of Memory.* New York: Random House.

Lopez, Martina. 1994. "Artist Statement and Portfolio." *Metamorphoses: Photography in the Electronic Age.* New York: Aperture Foundation. 12-17.

Lowenthal, David. 1996. *Possessed by the Past.* New York: Free.

Maier, Charles S. 1988. *The Unmasterable Past: History, Holocaust, and German National Identity.* Cambridge: Harvard UP.

Meyrowitz, Joshua. 1985. *No Sense of Place: The Impact of Electronic Media on Social Behavior.* New York: Oxford UP.

Morse, Margaret. 1994. "What Do Cyborgs Eat? Oral Logic in an Information Society." *Culture on the Brink: Ideologies of Technology.* Ed. G. Bender and T. Druckrey. Seattle: Bay. 157-204.

Simon, William, and John H. Gagnon. 1976. "The Anomie of Affluence." *American Journal of Sociology* 82: 356-78.

Stelarc. 1986. "Beyond the Body: Amplified Body, Laser Eyes, and Third Hand." *Contemporary Art: A Sourcebook of Artists' Writings.* Ed. K. Stiles and P. Selz. Berkeley: U of California P. 427-30.

Stiles, Kristine. 1996. "Art and Technology." *Contemporary Art: A Sourcebook of Artists' Writings.* Ed. K. Stiles and P. Selz . Berkeley: U of California P. 385-96.

Tomlinson, John. 1999. *Globalization and Culture.* Chicago: U of Chicago P.

Turkle, Sherry. 1995. *Life on the Screen: Identity in the Age of the Internet.* New York: Simon & Schuster.

Wiener, Norbert. 1948. *Cybernetics; or, Control and Communication in the Animal and the Machine.* New York: Wiley.

CONTRIBUTORS

Burton Beerman, Director, Mid-American Center for Contemporary Music, Bowling Green State University.

R. Brent Beerman, prizewinning Los Angeles playwright.

Yiwei Chen, Assistant Professor, Department of Psychology, Bowling Green State University.

Kathleen Dixon, Associate Professor of Philosophy, Bowling Green State University.

Dena Elisabeth Eber, Assistant Professor, School of Art, Bowling Green State University.

Kathryn Farr, Professor of Sociology, Portland State University.

Rebecca L. Green, Assistant Professor, School of Art, Bowling Green State University.

Celesta Haraszti, dancer/choreographer.

Arthur G. Neal, Adjunct Professor of Sociology, Portland State University.

Vivian Patraka, Director, Institute for the Study of Culture and Society, Bowling Green State University.

Patricia Reynaud, Associate Professor, Department of French and Italian, Miami University.